HOW AMERICA'S POLITICAL PARTIES CHANGE (AND HOW THEY DON'T)

MICHAEL BARONE

BOOKS

New York • London

First American edition published in 2019 by Encounter Books,
an activity of Encounter for Culture and Education, Inc.,
a nonprofit, tax-exempt corporation.
Encounter Books website address: www.encounterbooks.com

Manufactured in the United States and printed on
acid-free paper. The paper used in this publication meets
the minimum requirements of ANSI/NISO Z39.48–1992
(R 1997) (*Permanence of Paper*).

FIRST AMERICAN EDITION

LIBRARY OF CONGRESS CATALOGING-IN-PUBLICATION DATA
Names: Barone, Michael, author.
Title: How America's political parties change (and how they don't) /
by Michael Barone.
Description: New York : Encounter Books, 2019. |
Includes bibliographical references and index.
Identifiers: LCCN 2019013893 (print) | LCCN 2019016278 (ebook) |
ISBN 9781641770798 (ebook) | ISBN 9781641770781 (hardcover : alk. paper)
Subjects: LCSH: Political parties—United States—History. |
United States—Politics and government.
Classification: LCC JK2261 (ebook) | LCC JK2261 .B3444 2019 (print) |
DDC 324.273—dc23°LC record available at https://lccn.loc.gov/2019013893

Page design and composition: BooksByBruce.com

For Alex P.

CONTENTS

INTRODUCTION

Panic is a poor guide to reality. In the nine o'clock hour on the evening of November 8, 2016, as it became clear that Hillary Clinton was not going to win the electoral votes of Florida and Pennsylvania and that Donald Trump was going to be the 45th president of the United States, something like panic set in for millions of Americans and foreigners who had not until that point imagined that such an outcome was possible. Panicky predictions were made about what President Trump might do and about how our entire political system might be destabilized. Panicky predictions were made that huge shifts in voting behavior meant either that Republicans had gained forever a monopoly of white working-class voters—or that Republicans were doomed to be the minority party for the rest of history, if they were to remain an active political party at all.

For those of us with some years of experience observing postelection commentary, all this had a certain familiarity. I am old enough to have observed the predictions of the death of the Republican Party after the election of 1964 and of the permanent minority status of the Democratic Party after its electoral reverses in the 1980s and 1990s. I have read enough history to know how plausible such predictions were after the 60 to 34 percent defeat of the Democratic Party in 1920 and the 57 to 40 percent defeat of the Republican Party just twelve years later, in 1932.

In fact the change in party percentages between 2012 and 2016—or between any presidential election since 1996 and that of 2016—was minimal by historical standards. Donald Trump's percentage of the popular vote was 1 percent lower than Mitt Romney's in 2012, while Hillary Clinton's share was 3 percent lower than Barack Obama's that year. The most recent generation of our politics has been characterized by what I have called polarized partisan parity, to an extent that is arguably unprecedented in American history. There were far greater oscillations in party percentages between the elections of 1976 and 1980, for example, or between those of 1988 and 1992.

It's true that there were bigger shifts in the levels of support for each party's nominee by certain segments of the electorate—shifts that produced, to almost everyone's surprise, an Electoral College majority for Donald Trump—but these were not of unprecedented magnitude either. Trump, as compared with Romney or other recent Republican nominees, won fewer votes from white college graduates and additional votes—just a little more—from white non-college-graduates. But his losses among the former group cost him no electoral votes, while his gains among the latter netted him the 100 electoral votes of Florida, Pennsylvania, Ohio, Michigan, Wisconsin, Iowa, and the 2nd congressional district of Maine. His margins were small and arguably tenuous, as indicated by the net loss of 40 or 41 House seats by the Republican Party in 2018, as Republican House candidates failed to match Trump levels of support from non-college whites and, more significantly, suffered further losses among white college graduates.

The panicky responses are in need of perspective. In my commentary at public forums at the American Enterprise Institute and in my columns in the *Washington Examiner*, I have argued that we are not in the midst of a gigantic electoral upheaval but something more in the nature of a course correction and that our political parties have persisted and adapted through more daunting challenges. Americans seem to be placidly unaware that we have the oldest and third oldest political parties in the world, with the Democratic Party dating from the 1832 national convention that nominated Andrew Jackson for a second term and the Republican Party dating from 1854 protests against the Kansas-Nebraska Act allowing slavery in the territories. Their only competitor in longevity is the British Conservative Party (itself in a period of turmoil today), which its leading historian, Robert Blake, dates to reaction against the repeal of the Corn Laws in 1846. Parties as long-lasting as these, I submit, even as they shift positions in response to events and elections, represent something basic in the character of the nations they have governed with considerable and recurring success.

These arguments are hard to convey in short-form journalism and rapid-fire commentary. It is especially difficult to make reference to historic persons and events that are not immediately familiar even to generally well-informed citizens. Fortunately I have had the opportunity over the past two years to address them at greater length, in what I hope is an accessible manner however unfamiliar the material. One of my great pleasures in life is what I call my vagrant reading—prowling through books with no direct or immediate connection to my work—and among my favorite types of books are the slim volumes consisting of a few lectures by eminent historians like H. R. Trevor-Roper and J. H. Elliott, Bernard Bailyn and Edmund Morgan. There are few more delightful ways to spend an evening than settling into a comfortable chair and reading in one sitting a brilliant scholar's distillation of a lifetime of learning, enlivened by a gift for the arresting example. Such books are the models I had in mind when preparing these essays, versions of which were delivered as lectures.

My subject is the long history—and the striking resilience—of our two political parties. When I first started reading history as a child, I wondered why other sorts of parties—a socialist party, a progressive party, a traditionalist party, a religious party—had not developed in the United States. One answer is that our electoral system—the Electoral College, the single-member congressional (and senatorial) district—works powerfully against the emergence of such alternatives. This is one reason why this country did not spawn a major socialist party in the early twentieth century, as most European democracies did, and why the Progressive Party, led by America's leading vote-getter up to that point, Theodore Roosevelt, vanished less than half a dozen years after its second-place finish in the election of 1912.

But there is something more basic about our American parties, I came to think as I mulled their history, something fundamental to how the two of them together have for many years provided voters with a yin-and-yang alternative in what has always been a diverse nation—diverse regionally, economically, religiously, racially and ethnically, culturally—from its colonial beginnings. The Republican Party has always been formed around a core of people who are considered, by themselves and others, to be typical Americans, although they are never by themselves a majority: northern Protestants in the nineteenth century, married white people in the twenty-first. The Democratic Party has always been a combination, a coalition, of people who are not thought of, by themselves or others, as typical Americans, but who together often form a majority:

southern slaveholders and big-city Catholics in the nineteenth century, churchgoing and urban blacks and affluent urban and suburban liberals in the twenty-first.

Both parties have changed their policies, adapting to economic and demographic circumstances and to signals in the political marketplace. And both parties, in the process, have tended to provide a congenial (though sometimes very temporary) political home for the large majority of Americans over many years. The fact that they have been performing those functions for so long, under stress and despite massive setbacks, provides some basis for thinking that they will pass through the stress test being administered by Donald Trump, his Republican fans and critics, and his Democratic opponents, as they have passed through others even more stringent many times before. Perspective is a better guide to reality than panic.

I

The Parties in History

CHAPTER 1

Lessons from the Early Republic

The Democratic and Republican parties have persisted in unbroken chains extending now 187 and 165 years, respectively. This is despite predictions after every unfavorable election cycle of the extinction of one or the other, or of their replacement by some unnamed third party. How this unusual thing has come to happen is an interesting story, and may serve to calm some of the jangled nerves of those involved in and observing American politics today. It is a story of the parties' enduring character and pliable policies, of their adherence to principle and adaptation to circumstance, of successive challenge and response.

Let me illustrate by describing the first time I found myself in a quarrel with an eminent historian. I was a college freshman, and the historian was Arthur Schlesinger, Jr. The dispute concerned his first major work, *The Age of Jackson*, which was awarded a Pulitzer Prize in 1945 when Schlesinger was not yet thirty years old. *The Age of Jackson* is a beautifully written book, one that wanders beguilingly over the intellectual landscape and the demographic developments of the 1830s and 1840s. My quarrel was with Schlesinger's portrait of Andrew Jackson as a harbinger, a forerunner of "that Democratic president who would come a century later," Franklin Roosevelt. Schlesinger of course was a strong New Dealer and on multiple occasions a political propagandist, a spirited young man with a vested intellectual interest in establishing continuity between the slaveholder of the Hermitage and the squire of Hyde Park.

But as I knew from previous reading, Franklin Roosevelt stood for big government, deficit financing, and inflationary currency—while Jackson, as Schlesinger had to concede when he came to the specifics of policy—stood for pretty much the opposite. Government was an oppressor of the ordinary American, Jackson thought. He boasted of running budget surpluses that, briefly, eliminated the national debt. His mistrust of paper money amounted to hatred, and he triggered a financial panic by requiring buyers of federal lands to pay in gold (which Franklin Roosevelt banned).

Schlesinger glided over these contradictions, asserting that both of those Democratic presidents, a century apart, stood for "the little guy." Both, he pointed out with fair accuracy, were opposed and belittled by sophisticated operators in the great financial centers of their day, Philadelphia's Chestnut Street, New York's Wall Street—in the same supercilious way that Schlesinger was treated as a Harvard student at a time when most undergraduates were Republicans. Which led me, as a Harvard student at a time when most undergraduates were Democrats, to dismiss as partisan special pleading his argument that Jackson and Roosevelt stood for the same things.

CHAPTER 2

Adaptation

W hat I have come to believe, after many years of reading and reflection, is that America's two political parties have maintained, over their astonishingly long lifespans, their basic character, their political DNA. But each has done so only by adapting its policies and adjusting its personnel when faced with political circumstances threatening its viability. This is the process of challenge and response (to adopt the terms of the pseudo-historian Arnold Toynbee) that I will describe here, as it evolved over the first half of the history of the Republic.

Let me start by describing again what I believe to be the enduring character, the political DNA, of the two major American parties. The Democratic Party, from its beginnings in the 1830s, has always been a collection of out-groups, of demographic groups that have not been regarded by themselves or others as typically American but which, taken together—and it is almost always a problem holding them together—make up a majority of the nation. The Republican Party has always been formed around a core group considered to be typical Americans, but which by itself has never been a majority of the electorate and must attract others to the party's banner in order to win.

So if these parties have maintained their basic character, how did they shift so markedly on major issues? To go back to Arthur Schlesinger's example, how did the laissez-faire Democrats of the 1830s become the big-government Democrats of the 1930s? How did the activist-government Republican Party of the 1850s and 1860s become skeptical in the 1920s of the efficacy and desirability of government direction, decrying progressivism and proclaiming instead a return to normalcy?

The answer is that these changes came abruptly, suddenly—as abruptly and suddenly as these two parties had come into existence—in unusually turbulent times. Times of technological change, economic growth, demographic challenge, and geographical expansion. Times of distress, perhaps, but even more so, times of disruption. Times in which the appeal of existing political parties—Thomas Jefferson's dominant Republicans of the 1820s, Henry Clay's competitive Whigs of the 1840s— seem threatened and jeopardized by changes they had not anticipated.

The Democratic Party was formed at exactly the time that Alexis de Tocqueville was visiting the rapidly changing and growing nation he would describe in *Democracy in America*—including a foray into the wild and largely unsettled Michigan Territory. This was a time of frantic westward expansion, the creation of giant cotton plantations in the Mississippi Valley and the proliferation of schoolhouses and colleges in the Northwest Territory north of the Ohio River and flanking the Great Lakes, the efflorescence of the hundreds and thousands of voluntary associations that Tocqueville identified as the essence of the young democratic nation. In this dynamic, chaotic nation, Jackson's Democratic Party created connections between Tennessee and Pennsylvania, the frontier Northwest and the Manhattan docks, connections lubricated by the spoils of office and the promise of upward mobility through an articulated organization, in this case the Democratic Party.

The Republican Party sprang suddenly into existence in the 1850s, surely the most disruptive decade in the history of the Republic, less than a decade after its boundaries had spread tenuously across the continent, and at a time when immigration as a percentage of preexisting population was at the highest levels in history. Millions were streaming in speaking unfamiliar languages such as German and practicing unfamiliar faiths like Catholicism. The Cotton Kingdom that was coming into existence in 1832 was by 1854 an integral part of the largest and most lucrative business in the world, as millions of bales of cotton were shipped to the English textile mills in Lancashire. From northern ports, clipper ships—the fastest cargo sailing ships ever built—were fanning out across the globe in search of precious cargo, from tea to opium to whale oil. The invention of the telegraph and the development of railroads shrunk time and space in the rapidly industrializing Northeast and Midwest.

In the fast-growing North, the disintegration of the Whig Party and the increasing southern orientation of the Democrats created a vacuum and led to a chaotic competition for the support of similar constituencies between immigration restrictionists (the American or Know-Nothing Party), alcohol prohibitionists (the Prohibition Party), and opponents of the extension of slavery into the territories (the Republican Party). Out of this competition the Republicans emerged the winners, but only just. They won their first presidential election after nominating a candidate who did not favor cutting off immigration (but was of colonial stock from Kentucky), did not favor banning alcohol (but did not drink), and opposed abolition of slavery (though he abhorred it). The American political system, or the candidate's campaign apparatchiks at the Republican National Convention in Chicago (the first ever held there), managed to produce a nominee who straddled party divisions and also, incidentally, had a piercing intellect and uncommon moral strength. The selection of Abraham Lincoln, together with the penetrating intelligence and sublime prudence of the Founders, provides the strongest evidence for the argument that a divine providence had a hand in shaping this nation.

The Democratic and Republican parties had been created as political responses to challenges posed by socioeconomic and demographic change. For a quarter of a century, the battles between them were conducted on familiar ideological and demographic ground, despite vast westward migration and substantial immigration and technological innovation symbolized by the electric light and the telephone. Voting in every election was highly correlated with opinion on the Civil War. It was a time of polarized partisan parity—reminiscent of the last two decades—in which election results varied widely only in southern states, depending on whether blacks, then heavily Republican, were allowed to vote. The decade of the 1880s, when the disenfranchisement of blacks was largely complete, featured astonishingly static partisan alignments, with the nation almost exactly evenly divided between the parties—a situation not seen again until the first years of this century. In the three presidential elections of the 1880s, both parties' nominees received between 47.8 and 48.9 percent of the popular votes—48 percent and 49 percent rounded off. So evenly balanced was the partisan division in this period that the Republicans usually held the presidency and the Democrats usually won majorities in the House of Representatives—the opposite of the partisan situation that is familiar today.

Republicans in this period, centered on a core of northern white Protestants, were the party favoring nationally uniform policies and a vigorous federal government exercising authority over discordant states that practiced racial discrimination or imposed market-interfering regulation. Their attempts at Reconstruction in the South failed, but they succeeded in reestablishing the gold standard and currency stability, and the protection of property rights by the courts—policies that fostered enormous economic growth and amazing technological innovation. The Democrats, centered on disparate constituencies of southern whites and northern immigrant Catholics, were the party of regionalism and laissez faire, free trade, and parsimonious government spending. They were happy to tolerate both segregation and the saloon: something for the white South, something for Irish immigrants in the big cities. In this regard, they resembled the Liberal Party of Britain, which backed free trade and low taxes and was sympathetic to ethnic out-groups, as Robert L. Kelley documents in *The Transatlantic Persuasion*.[1]

By 1890, a quarter century had passed since the surrender at Appomattox, and more than one-third of voters had no living memory of the Civil War. The rapidly growing cities had been hit by waves of strikes and violent protests. Drought and crop failures struck the newly settled Great Plains. Railroads and giant corporations seemed to have gained monopoly control over economic markets at the expense of consumers, employees, and especially farmers, still the majority of the nation's workers. The huge fortunes being accumulated by capitalists—and not yet being devoted in large part to creative and productive philanthropy, as so many later would be—seemed to mock American traditions of equality. In this situation, support for both major parties started to decline and a new Populist Party sprang into existence in the boom-and-bust states of the West. In 1892, a Populist presidential candidate won 9 percent of the national popular vote and carried the electoral votes of North Dakota,

Kansas, Colorado, Idaho, and Nevada. Partisan churn upset congressional voting patterns, producing huge Republican losses in 1890 and even larger Democratic losses in 1894.

In 1896, William Jennings Bryan, a 36-year-old former congressman from Nebraska, won the Democratic nomination by calling for "free silver"—abandonment of the hard-money gold standard—and absorbed the Populist Party. The eloquent Bryan barnstormed the nation and for a time seemed headed for victory, even though he was opposed by the incumbent Democratic president, Grover Cleveland. But the Republican nominee, William McKinley—a Civil War veteran, longtime congressman, and former governor of Ohio—adjusted his strategy, framing his support of the gold standard and a protective tariff and his friendliness toward labor unions as guarantees of good wages for the working man: a story well told in Karl Rove's 2015 book, *The Triumph of William McKinley*.[2] McKinley carried the popular vote 51 to 47 percent—but Rove argues persuasively that Bryan was leading during much of the campaign and that McKinley's victory was anything but inevitable. His argument is strengthened by the fact that the patterns of regional and demographic support were far different from the post–Civil War norm and would be roughly replicated for the next dozen or so years. Bryan ran far ahead of earlier Democrats from Kansas and Nebraska on west through the Rocky Mountains to the Pacific Northwest. But in an industrializing and urbanizing nation, McKinley ran far ahead of previous Republicans in New England, New York, Pennsylvania, and Illinois, in the booming industrial large cities and factory towns like McKinley's own Canton, Ohio. Civil War voting patterns receded: McKinley was competitive, as Republicans would be until the 1930s, in the Upper South—Kentucky, Tennessee, North Carolina, Virginia, and West Virginia.

The election of 1896 set into place new voting patterns and new issue positions, which would mostly remain in place for a long generation, indeed for a longer period than the 25 years between Appomattox and 1890. The core of the Republican Party was redefined as the northern small-town and city dweller, while the dominant out-groups of the Democratic Party were the Deep South and the West, especially the Rocky Mountains and also the Great Plains states west of the Missouri River. Democrats lost ground as compared with the post–Civil War period in large cities like New York and Chicago.

The waning of Civil War loyalties was accompanied by a shrinking of the electorate, not only by the disenfranchisement of blacks in the South, but also by progressive measures that supposedly put more power in the hands of the people. The old one-party ballots handed out at polling places were replaced by the Australian ballot, compiled by state governments and including all parties, to be cast in the privacy of a voting booth. Primary elections allowed voters rather than party leaders to select parties' general-election candidates, though in many cases party leaders still exerted dominant influence. Similarly, initiative and referendum—plebiscites on policy—promoted some popular innovative policies, but also were manipulated by party leaders and economic interest groups. Literacy tests and poll taxes imposed in the South to prevent blacks from voting blocked many nonaffluent whites as well. Civil service reforms, passed federally in 1883, reduced the number of politicos motivated by lust for lucrative office. Voter participation never again reached the levels of the 1840s to 1890s; indeed the percentage of those eligible who voted in 1908 has never been equaled in the 110 years since.

If the empowerment of ordinary people over politicians was only partial, there was a stronger and more successful movement of national elites seeking national standardization, as the historian Robert Wiebe has documented, a trend more congenial to Republicans than Democrats, and exemplified by the founding of groups such as the American Bar Association and the American Medical Association, headquartered in Chicago when it seemed likely to become the nation's largest city as well as its dominant railroad junction. Perhaps coincidentally, the period also saw elite dominance in the White House—the Harvard, Yale, Princeton presidencies of Theodore Roosevelt, William Howard Taft, and Woodrow Wilson, respectively, and the unsuccessful attempts of Harvard-educated newspaper scions like William Randolph Hearst and Robert McCormick to vault into higher office as well.

Another antidemocratic byproduct of the Progressive Era was the congressional seniority system adopted in 1910. This was the project of members who were first elected in 1898 (the first year in which a majority of House members were reelected and thus had much seniority), but were nonetheless passed over for leadership positions by the Republican leadership. It was adopted by Democrats as well, and longtime Speaker Sam Rayburn of Texas, first elected in 1912, almost always deferred to seniority until his death in 1961. Its effect was to freeze in positions of power small-town Republicans from the Midwest and the Northeast and small-town Democrats from the South: a classic example of a reform championed by progressives that enhanced the power of their ideological adversaries.

During this period, the Republican Party continued to stand for nationalizing policies—the tariff, maintained despite the qualms of Roosevelt and Taft; the Sherman Antitrust Act, passed by a Republican government in 1890 and employed vigorously by those two Republican presidents; railroad regulations, increased by Republican congresses and presidents; the creation of multiple national parks and monuments, the building of dams and land reclamation projects. This was not laissez-faire government.

Democrats, influenced by Bryan's populist platform, also started entertaining proposals for national economic regulation, much like the contemporaneous Liberal Party government in Britain. In New York—still the nation's largest city and remaining so thanks to the throngs of immigrants from eastern and southern Europe who settled there after passing through Ellis Island from 1892 to 1914—the Tammany boss Charles F. Murphy encouraged young legislative leaders like Al Smith and Robert Wagner to pass legislation on wages and hours and worker safety. The pursuit of such policies influenced Democrats when they finally broke through the McKinley majorities in the 1912 election, in which Theodore Roosevelt challenged his handpicked successor, William Howard Taft, and the Democratic nominee, Woodrow Wilson, the two-year governor of New Jersey.

Wilson was elected in 1912 with 42 percent of the popular vote. Democrats passed their own antitrust act, established the Federal Reserve system (divided into eleven regional banks in the interest of decentralization), and created the Federal Trade Commission—the latter a month after World War I broke out in Europe. The United States had not faced the challenge of responding to a major European war for 99 years, and the Wilson administration was at first determined to stay out of it. That resolve was tested in May 1915, when a German submarine sank the ocean liner *Lusitania* off the coast of Ireland and some 120 Americans died. Wilson then demanded "strict accountability" from Germany for any infringement of American rights. In response, William

Jennings Bryan, who favored strict neutrality, resigned from his post as secretary of state.

Wilson ran for reelection in 1916 as the president who "kept us out of war," and he won a narrow victory: 49 to 46 percent in the popular vote, 277 to 254 in the Electoral College, carrying the entire South and almost all the West but losing every state in the Northeast and the industrial Midwest except New Hampshire and Ohio. This was just a slight improvement on William Jennings Bryan's three electoral performances, and in the electorally crucial large states in the Midwest, Wilson's percentages were uncannily similar to Bryan's twenty years before.

In early 1917, Germany announced it would resume unrestricted submarine warfare, and a decoded telegram from the German foreign minister, Arthur Zimmermann, revealed a promise to Mexico to return the American southwestern territories lost in 1848 in exchange for support against the United States. Wilson then asked Congress for a declaration of war. This was not uncontroversial. Six senators and 50 representatives voted no; 39 of the 56 were from the Midwest, mainly from the area heavily populated by German and Scandinavian Americans—Wisconsin, Minnesota, Iowa, and the Dakotas. The Wilson administration launched an offensive at home against things deemed German. Press censorship was imposed, and opponents of involvement in the war were imprisoned under a stringent Espionage Act. The American war effort lasted nineteen months, and American troops were engaged in major fighting for little more than a year, but some 116,000 Americans died in the war and 204,000 were wounded.

The aftermath of the war was even more unsettling. An influenza epidemic killed more than half a million Americans between 1918 and 1920. The economy was dizzyingly unsettled, with zooming inflation and then a sharp recession. Labor union strikes, sometimes violent, were more frequent than at any previous time. Americans were sent to Russia to fight the Communists, who for some moments seemed on the verge of taking over Hungary and Germany as well. Fighting raged on for years in Poland, Turkey, and the Middle East. At home, radicals set off deadly bombs at the attorney general's Washington home and on Wall Street in front of the New York Stock Exchange. Wilson, campaigning unsuccessfully for adoption without reservations of his Versailles Treaty and its League of Nations, collapsed from a stroke in

September 1919 and was disabled and out of public view for most of the rest of his second term.

This disorder presented a massive challenge to Wilson's Democratic Party, which failed to respond effectively. Wilson's war policies antagonized German, Scandinavian, and Irish American voters and western voters generally. The passage of Prohibition, imposed during wartime and made permanent by ratification of the 18th Amendment, antagonized many urbanites. The passage of the 19th Amendment, requiring women's suffrage nationally, antagonized urban Democrats. Disillusion and fear produced an enormous swing against Wilson and progressivism, toward Warren Harding, the Republican, and his "back to normalcy" campaign in 1920. Harding won the popular vote by 60 to 34 percent and the electoral vote by 404 to 127, delivering to Democrats the most devastating popular-vote defeat ever suffered by either of America's two major parties.

Harding carried every non-Confederate state except Kentucky (which he lost by 4,017 votes) and carried Tennessee as well. He carried Germano-Scandinavian states, where opposition to World War I had been strongest, with more than 70 percent, and he carried New England states, where support for the war had been strongest, with more than 65 percent. He carried the vast majority of rural and small-town counties outside the South, and he carried immigrant-thronged and industrial big cities—Boston, Philadelphia, Pittsburgh, Cleveland, Cincinnati, Detroit, Chicago, Milwaukee, Minneapolis, St. Louis, and all five boroughs of New York City.

As the 1920s went on, Republicans seemed to provide proper stewardship of the federal government, with tax cuts and budget reform, while the Democrats seemed fearsomely split between their southern wing and the Ellis Island immigrants of the big cities. Republicans were seen as sufficiently watchful of big corporations while also encouraging technological innovation and economic growth. Republican candidates carried great industrial cities—Philadelphia, Pittsburgh, Detroit, Chicago, and St. Louis—in just about every presidential election between 1896 and 1928 except in the three-way split of 1912. Republicans even carried New York City over its Tammany Hall Democratic machine in 1896, 1908, 1920, and 1924.

In democratic nations, any party that wins by such a large margin

has difficulty maintaining its dominance. A very large coalition inevitably contains groups with different goals, and Republicans in the 1920s
included progressives and farm-belt members bent first on maintaining
and then on resurrecting the Wilson administration's wartime farm
subsidies, originally imposed to encourage production for America's
European wartime allies but persisting to this day—which illustrates
the difficulty of eliminating government largesse. These progressives
resisted some administration policies in Congress and in 1924 supported
the Progressive Party candidacy of the elderly Senator Robert LaFollette,
who carried his home state of Wisconsin and came very close to carrying Minnesota and North Dakota as well—the Germano-Scandinavian
states which, like LaFollette, opposed entry into World War I.

Republican presidential nominees continued nonetheless to win by
large margins over Democrats—Calvin Coolidge by 54 to 29 percent in
1924, Herbert Hoover by 58 to 41 percent in 1928. The out-groups that
together had produced victories for Woodrow Wilson in the 1910s were
in irreconcilable conflict in the 1920s: southern Protestants backed
Prohibition and racial segregation, northern big-city Democrats opposed
Prohibition and backed labor unions. At the 1924 Democratic National
Convention, a vote to condemn the Ku Klux Klan was defeated by a hair,
and it took 103 ballots to choose a presidential nominee: John W. Davis,
a Wall Street lawyer and former West Virginia congressman. Al Smith,
the governor of New York, led but fell short of the required two-thirds in
the 86th to 93rd and the 100th and 101st ballots. Four years later, Smith
was nominated on the first ballot. His Catholic faith repelled many
otherwise loyal Democrats in the South and the Midwest, but attracted
Catholic and Jewish immigrants to the polls in the Northeast and the
industrial Midwest; he ran much better than other 1920s Democrats in
the Germano-Scandinavian states, especially among German Catholics.
Smith lost the electoral votes of eight southern states, but gained those
of Massachusetts and Rhode Island and came within 2 percent of carrying New York.

It is a moot historical question whether and how the Democrats
would probably have eventually mastered the challenge posed by the
collapse of support for Woodrow Wilson and his policies. During the
1920s, they elected governors and senators in many states their presidential candidates failed to carry, including such large states as New

York, Massachusetts, Ohio, and Michigan. Democratic politicians not called on to defend a national leader were free to adapt to local terrain, as the Democratic Party had done through most of its history, and also to emphasize their personal appeal. Republicans had maintained a hold on the White House for sixteen years starting in 1896, until a split among their leaders allowed Democrats to win; and then after regaining the presidency in 1920 they maintained a stronger hold on it for twelve years more. But the collapse of the national economy in the years after the October 1929 stock market crash ended Republicans' tenure and thrust the party into minority status and into a challenge as severe as that which the Democrats had been facing over the preceding dozen years.

I leave the story of that challenge and response to the subsequent essays. On the day of the stock market crash, the Democratic Party had been in existence for 97 years, the Republican Party for 75, and despite predictions of their imminent demise, they have both been around now for another 90 years. Neither, I would argue, is in as dire a condition as the Democrats seemed to be in 1920, and in the 1930s the Democrats won overwhelming victories in presidential and congressional elections. After the 2014 election, Republicans held more congressional and legislative seats than they have had since 1929, and yet Democrats have won four of the last seven presidential elections and popular-vote pluralities—not majorities, but pluralities—in two more. In fact, only in three of those seven presidential elections has a candidate won more than 50 percent of the popular vote, and in two cases they won just 51 percent. There has been much more stability in these voting patterns than in the 1970s and 1980s.

Our current political situation thus resembles the polarized partisan parity so apparent in the 1880s. Republicans have won House majorities in ten of the thirteen congressional elections starting with 1994, with a swing toward Democrats in 2006 and 2008; and in those ten elections the Republican percentage of the House popular vote has varied between 48 and 51 percent and the Democratic percentage between 44 and 49 percent—a very narrow range indeed. And as in the 1880s, these strong partisan preferences are based not so much on economic status, but on deeply held beliefs around which people have lived—and risked—their lives, beliefs that are not lightly cast aside.

Our pundit class today, of which I am a member, considers the almost entirely unexpected election of Donald Trump to be an upheaval of continental proportions. And of course it will have consequences (as compared with the expected victory of Hillary Clinton) which have only begun to appear. But the percentage of voters who switched from one party to the other—mainly white college graduates switching from Republicans to Hillary Clinton, and white non-college-graduates switching from Democrats to Donald Trump—is actually very small when considered in historical perspective. Both parties face challenges. But neither party faces challenges comparable to that faced by both parties in the 1890s, or by the Democrats in the 1920s, or by the Republicans in the 1930s. Such a challenge may come sooner or later, but it hasn't yet.

CHAPTER 3

Lessons from the Last Century

One of the facts about American politics seldom mentioned or even noticed is the great age—and great durability—of our two major political parties. The Democratic Party, formed in 1832, is the oldest political party in the world. The Republican Party, formed in 1854, is the third oldest. In the 187 and 165 years since their foundings, there have been frequent proclamations that one or the other of these two major parties was on the brink of breakup, was headed to oblivion, or was on its way to that graveyard of parties where the Whigs and the Federalists ended up after only twenty-some years of struggle. In nations with shorter histories of democratic politics, dozens of political parties have come and gone. But the American Democratic and Republican parties have managed to stick around for the better part of two centuries.

They have done so despite receiving rebuffs and rebukes vastly more devastating than what either has faced in the last several decades. Each received its most serious reverse in the early years of the twentieth century, a reverse that might have sent it speeding into nonexistence. Yet both not only survived, but also went on to win massive victories and, even more frequently, to significantly affect public policy. If politics is a survival of the fittest, both parties proved themselves fit to survive.

One of those electoral disasters is familiar to even the most casual student of American political history, the defeat of the incumbent president, Herbert Hoover, in 1932, the first of five consecutive presidential defeats for the Republican Party. That year also saw the beginning of almost a half century in which Democrats usually held majorities in both houses of Congress: for 44 out of 48 years. These top-line results inspired and give credence to the long-taught lesson that the 1932 election ushered in a long generation of natural Democratic majorities.

The other electoral disaster is less familiar, not widely taught, brushed aside as an exception rather than a rule, and considered a diversion from the main line of history. Recounting it has had little appeal to generations of partisan Democratic and ideologically progressive historians. It happened only twelve years further back in time than the Great Depression and the launching of the New Deal, but even as we approach its centennial it seems much more distant in time. It occurred in an America before the coming of radio and talking movies, where automobiles and refrigerators were unusual rather than universal. In some ways this period seems closer to the Civil War, which was a half century in the past, than to World War II, which was a quarter century in the future.

The defeat of the party of President Woodrow Wilson in 1920 was the first of three resounding presidential defeats for the Democratic Party. That year also saw the beginning of a decade in which Republicans had overwhelming margins in both houses of Congress, with a near-monopoly of seats outside the South. By some metrics, the political dominance of the Republican Party in the decade starting in 1920 was greater than that of the Democratic Party in the decade after 1932. Franklin Roosevelt beat Herbert Hoover in 1932 by a landslide popular-vote margin of 57 to 40 percent. But in 1920, Warren Harding beat James Cox by an even greater landslide, a popular-vote margin of 60 to 34 percent. Cox was by no means a negligible figure, but a three-term governor of the pivotal state of Ohio and a media baron whose surviving daughter, Anne Cox Chambers, today is a multibillionaire. (Both vice presidential nominees in 1920 were future presidents: Calvin Coolidge, who succeeded Harding after he died, and then was elected by a wide margin in 1924, and Franklin Roosevelt.)

Republicans carried the popular vote in the three presidential elections of 1920, 1924, and 1928 by an average margin of 58 to 35 percent. This is a wider margin than the 55 to 40 percent average by which

Democrats carried the popular vote in the three presidential elections of 1932, 1936, and 1940. The contrast also appears in congressional elections: in the five elections from 1920 to 1928, Republicans carried the popular vote for the House by an average margin of 56 to 41 percent; in the five elections from 1932 to 1940, Democrats' average margin in the popular vote for the House was 53 to 43 percent. Even in the 1930 election, which produced an almost exactly evenly split House, Republicans carried the popular vote by 53 to 45 percent, nearly the same as the Democrats' average margin in the next five elections.

The 1920s have been treated by American historians as a holiday from history, a decade in which carefree flappers sipped bathtub gin and Americans partied until the inevitable crash—the Great Depression—and the morning-after hangover. But the economic advances of the 1920s were not illusory: the advances in mass manufacturing, the networks of paved roads filled with family cars and fleets of trucks, the arrival of electric refrigerators and clothes washers, a giant expansion of retail outlets, the spread of radio into every electrified home and of movies into every city and town. And the public appeal of the Republican Party's "normalcy," a word introduced into political discourse by the former journalist Warren Harding in his 1920 campaign, was not illusory either. It represented a sharp reaction against—a repudiation of—the progressivism and globalism championed in stirring tones by President Woodrow Wilson, a president repudiated more thoroughly than any other in our post–Civil War history.

To understand Wilson's debacle, we need to go back to the beginning of the 1910s, a decade which saw the closest challenge to the two-party system since the 1850s, when the Republican Party emerged from years of political maelstrom as the only serious competitor to the party then called the Democracy. The competition between Republicans and Democrats continued for half a century, interrupted only momentarily by the emergence of the Populist Party in 1892, which was absorbed by the Democratic Party when it nominated William Jennings Bryan in 1896. In the third of a century before 1896, the two parties were in electoral parity, with Republicans holding the White House and Democrats the House of Representatives most of the time, usually with tenuous margins for both the presidency and the House. But starting in 1896, when Bryan was soundly defeated by William McKinley, Republicans won four straight presidential elections by wide margins and held solid margins in the House until 1910.

The Republican Party continued to stand for nationalizing policies and an energetic federal government, supporting a protective tariff, employing the Sherman Antitrust Act (passed by a Republican Congress and signed by a Republican president in 1890), creating national parks and constructing multiple dams. The Democratic Party, a believer in laissez-faire economics until Bryan, chimed in with proposals for national economic regulation. These were the years dubbed the Progressive Era, a time of suddenly enormous business corporations, when academics and intellectual journalists called for a more vigorous government with organized bureaucracies commanded by supposedly apolitical experts. Politicians followed the progressive fashion: Robert LaFollette, a conventional Republican congressman from Wisconsin in the 1890s and governor from 1900 to 1905, launched regulatory bureaucracies designed and staffed by professors from the university across town in Madison. In Washington as a senator he bucked the Republican leadership. Theodore Roosevelt was widely considered a progressive throughout his presidency, from 1901 to 1909, and so was his handpicked successor, at least in his first years in office.

CHAPTER 4

Challenging the Two-Party System

Two new parties rose suddenly to challenge the duopoly. One was the Progressive Party, which advocated some of the professors' programs like social insurance and campaign finance regulation. But in 1912 it was a personal vehicle for Theodore Roosevelt, who after returning from tours of Europe and Africa decided that William Howard Taft was insufficiently progressive—even though Taft filed more antitrust suits than TR, pursued conservation policies, and called successfully for a federal income tax. Roosevelt won six out of nine of the newly created presidential primaries (another progressive reform) but was defeated at the Republican National Convention in June, and was nominated by a hastily called Progressive National Convention in August.

As a party, the Progressives had formidable assets, more than any other third-party movement since the 1850s: a label widely praised in national media, a nominee who in his 1904 campaign had won what was then the highest percentage of the popular vote in history (56 percent), and a ticket of candidates for the House of Representatives in a majority of congressional districts. Roosevelt finished second in the popular vote (27 percent) and in electoral votes (with 88, and coming within 5 percent of carrying 84 more). Taft finished third, with nearly as many popular votes, 23 percent, but only the 8 electoral votes of Utah and Vermont, though he came within 5 percent of carrying 41 more from six states. The Progressive Party's candidates for House of Representatives got more than 5 percent of the votes in 213 of the 435 congressional districts, and in 213 of the 306 outside the South.

If there was ever a chance since the 1850s for a third party to break through to major-party status, this was it. Yet only a handful of Progressive congressional candidates (some of whom were cross-endorsed by the old parties) won their races, and by 1916 the party had almost completely vanished.

The other challenge came from the Socialist Party, which hoped to emulate the success of counterparts in Europe. The British Labour Party was formed in 1900 and elected two members of Parliament that year, gaining enough strength to head the government in 1924. The Australian Labour Party was founded in 1901 and immediately won 14 of 75 seats in the House of Representatives that year. The French Socialist Party was founded in 1902 and included deputies such as Jean Jaurès, who had been elected as long before as 1885. The grandfather of them all was the German Social Democratic Party, founded in 1875 and running parliamentary candidates since 1890; it won more votes than any other party in 1912. It looked like the newly enfranchised urban working classes in Europe would be swept up with enthusiasm for socialism. America seemed to be lagging; in 1906 the German Marxist Werner Sombart wrote a book entitled *Why is there no Socialism in the United States?* But by 1912 the Socialists in America had an attractive candidate, Eugene Debs, a labor union leader from Terre Haute, Indiana, who had won 3 percent of the presidential popular vote in the previous two elections. With great masses of eastern and southern European immigrants in the big northern cities and an increasing mass of industrial workers in their giant factories, the Socialists hoped that a third Debs candidacy could produce the kind of socialist takeoff that others had produced in Europe.

Debs won 6 percent of the popular vote in 1912, a peak that the Socialists never again reached, and the Progressive Party was gone within four years. One clue to the demise of both parties is that neither one aroused mass enthusiasm, in spite of Debs's appeal to class interests and Theodore Roosevelt's declaration that "We stand at Armageddon and battle for the Lord!" Voter turnout in 1912 sagged rather than boomed. In these years, segregationists were eviscerating black turnout and cutting white turnout in the South with literacy tests and poll taxes, while progressives in the North issued restrictions designed to limit the ability of political machines to turn out partisans. Nationally, turnout was up only 1 percent, mostly in the West; it was lower than in the conventional two-party contest of 1908 in most states east of the Rockies. The image of an enthusiastic electorate surging to the polls for progressives is at odds with the facts.

Significantly, little of Debs's support came from the growing urban proletariat. His best statewide showings, 16 percent, came in Oklahoma, newly admitted to the Union in 1907, and extremely sparsely populated Nevada, in the recently settled West, which had been the nation's most volatile region in Republican-Democratic competition since the 1890s. He did especially well in mining towns and lumber centers. In urban centers his best showing by far was the 27 percent he won in Milwaukee, whose heavily German American voters had already elected two Socialists: Victor Berger to Congress and Emil Seidel as mayor in 1910. (Milwaukee would have Socialist mayors in 1910–12, 1916–40, and 1948–60.) Debs won 18 percent in Dayton, 15 percent in Pittsburgh, 14 percent in Toledo and Oakland, and 10 to 12 percent in Cleveland, Chicago, Minneapolis, San Francisco, Cleveland, Columbus, and Seattle. But he won only 5 percent in New York and even less in Philadelphia, Baltimore, and Boston.

The Progressives virtually disappeared by 1916, when Roosevelt refused their nomination and instead supported the Republican nominee, Charles Evans Hughes, and only a handful of Progressives ran for Congress. (The Progressive label was resuscitated in 1924 and 1948 for candidacies that were essentially personal, with only regional and ethnic appeal: Robert LaFollette in the German and Scandinavian American Upper Midwest, Henry Wallace in heavily Jewish New York City.) As for the Socialists, Debs did not run in 1916, but in 1920, while in federal prison for delivering an antiwar speech, he won more than 900,000 votes—which amounted to only 3 percent of total votes in an electorate that had been enlarged by women's suffrage. The Socialists supported LaFollette's Progressive candidacy in 1924. Their candidate in 1928, Norman Thomas, won just 1 percent, and only 2 percent in the Depression year of 1932. By then, the party's support was concentrated in New York City and Milwaukee, with little remnant of the support it had won two decades before in Oklahoma or the West.

CHAPTER 5

The Wilson Years

The Republican-Progressive split and the slight rise of the Socialists in 1912 left plenty of room for the Democratic presidential candidate, Woodrow Wilson. The first and thus far the only Ph.D. president, Wilson won with only 42 percent of the popular vote (and 50 percent or more only in the eleven states of the Confederacy), but 435 of 531 electoral votes (309 of them from non-Confederate states). Democrats also won substantial majorities in both the House and the Senate: this was the first time Democrats held all three since 1893–95, which in turn had been the first time since 1857–59. Wilson grew up in the South and was old enough to remember General Sherman's troops storming Columbia, South Carolina; and for the first time in six decades, a presidential administration and congressional leaders had a pronounced southern accent.

The Wilson administration governed, energetically, in the progressive vogue of the day. Democrats levied the first income tax since the Civil War, passed the Clayton Antitrust Act (named after a congressman from Eufala, Alabama), created the Federal Trade Commission, and established the Federal Reserve. The outbreak of World War I in Europe in August 1914 was followed by a burst of prosperity, as the British and the French purchased American armaments and farm products, adding vigor to the rapidly expanding industrial economy symbolized by Henry

Ford's granting a $5 daily wage to his mostly unskilled workers in his new Highland Park plant.

Wilson first resolved to stay out of the European war, until the sinking of the *Lusitania* led him to demand accountability from Germany. In 1916 he ran for reelection as the president who "kept us out of war," winning by 49 to 46 percent in the popular vote and 277 to 254 in electoral votes. He carried the whole South and most of the West, but lost in most of the Northeast and the industrial Midwest. After Germany announced a resumption of unrestricted submarine warfare, and it emerged that Germany was seeking an alliance with Mexico against the United States, Wilson asked Congress to declare war on Germany—a request opposed by six senators and 50 representatives, mainly from the Upper Midwest states with large numbers of German and Scandinavian Americans.

The Democratic Congress promptly passed stringent laws on espionage and sedition. Antiwar protesters, including the Socialist presidential candidate Eugene Debs, were imprisoned. The Wilson administration launched an aggressive campaign of propaganda and press censorship, and encouraged a *kulturkampf* (not called that, of course) against all things regarded as German: German language instruction was banned, sauerkraut was renamed liberty cabbage, German musical and community organizations were shut down. Though American involvement in major fighting was relatively brief, it resulted in twice as many casualties as all previous foreign wars combined.

In its first five years, the Wilson administration seemed to bear out the argument of progressive intellectuals that bureaucracies headed by credentialed experts could guide and control an increasingly enormous and complex society in the new industrial age. The administration appeared to provide such guidance, and it made similar moves during the war: nationalizing railroads in December 1917 and telephone and telegraph lines in July 1918; fixing the price of coal and paying subsidies to farmers whose produce was needed to help feed Europe. "I am perfectly sure that the state has got to control everything that everybody needs and uses," Wilson told friends later.[3]

Then, suddenly, as American soldiers endured stressful combat and started dying in large numbers, things seemed to spin out of control. The Treaty of Brest-Litovsk between Germany and Russia's revolutionary Communist regime in March 1918 unleashed German forces to launch an offensive that drove the Allies almost back to Paris and left Allied victory far from assured. Nature was hostile as well. An influenza virus, first observed in early 1918 in Camp Funston, Kansas, broke out in a second, more virulent wave in September and killed about 675,000 Americans at home and overseas, most of them young adults, over the next nine months. About half of those deaths occurred in a ten-week period in fall 1918, as the war ground on and President Wilson refused to take actions that would interfere with the war effort. An armistice and German surrender ended trench warfare in November 1918, but conflict continued. Communist revolutionaries briefly took control of Munich and Budapest and threatened other capitals. American and British troops were fighting alongside the White Army trying to oust Communists from Russia. Fighting raged between Greece and Turkey, and Wilson considered a request for an American protectorate for Armenians.

Wilson went to Paris to negotiate a peace treaty, becoming the first incumbent president to visit Europe. He brought no Republicans with him, though they had won narrow congressional majorities in the 1918 elections and their support would be needed to get the necessary two-thirds Senate approval of any treaty. Wilson had set forth an idealistic version in his January 1918 Fourteen Points speech, including "open covenants of peace, openly arrived at," national self-determination of peoples, and a League of Nations authorized to act militarily against aggression. But the agreement he reached in secret negotiations and signed at Versailles in June 1919 fell short of those goals. The chairman of the Senate Foreign Relations Committee, Henry Cabot Lodge, announced that he would not support ratification without reservations particularly to preserve Congress's constitutional prerogative of declaring war. Wilson refused to compromise, and he traveled by train around the country delivering stirring speeches in favor of the treaty and the League. But he collapsed after a stroke in September 1919 and remained in seclusion in the White House, inaccessible to officials and reporters, until a partial recovery in March 1920.

Disorder swept the country in different ways in 1919. Inflation kept roaring at wartime levels, influenza spread across the country, and race riots broke out in Washington, Chicago, and more than 25 other American cities. Seattle, a center of the radical International Workers of the World, was shut down by a general strike in February 1919, and that year saw more labor union strikes, involving one out of five American workers, than any other in American history. The United Mine Workers struck the coal industry, employees struck U.S. Steel, and there was a police strike in Boston, quelled by Governor Calvin Coolidge's refusal to negotiate. Socialist revolutionaries mailed multiple bombs on May Day, and in June a bomb was detonated outside the Washington home of the attorney general, A. Mitchell Palmer. Americans had reason to fear that the revolutionary Communist movement so successful abroad would come here too. Historians with the benefit of hindsight have scoffed at this "Red Scare," but at a time when the czarist Russian Empire, the German Empire, and the Austro-Hungarian Empire had been overthrown within the past two years, it was not apparent that America was immune. Palmer and federal agents, including the young J. Edgar Hoover, staged so-called Red Raids starting in November 1919, and in January 1920 they arrested some 5,000 radicals. In spring 1920, inflation turned to deflation as wholesale prices peaked and the Dow Jones average dropped 39 percent. By the end of 1920, unemployment—then not officially measured—was up to about 20 percent.

Americans understandably were stunned by the dizziness of these events, so totally unanticipated just four years before. The progressive experts who were supposed to be controlling events seemed surprised and stunned too. The progressive president whose stentorian oratory seemed to guide the nation was now huddling incapacitated and mute in the White House, his promise to make the world safe for democracy unfulfilled. As Arthur Herman has written, "In short, all that Wilson's Progressivism had promised—racial harmony, better pay and a higher standard of living for the average worker and the little guy, a booming but more just economy carefully micromanaged by the experts at the Federal Reserve, *and* staying out of war—had turned out to be lies."[4]

Wilson, incredibly, contemplated running for a third term in 1920, even though he was obviously weaker than in 1916, when he had been reelected by just 49 to 46 percent—a percentage not much higher than those of William Jennings Bryan in 1896 and 1900. After the disorder and disappointments of 1919 and 1920, not only Wilson but his party and the broader progressive movement with which he identified were overwhelmingly repudiated. Wilson's war policy—fighting with Britain and against Germany—angered German, Scandinavian, and Irish American voters. So did Prohibition, made permanent with the 18th Amendment, though it was never accepted or effectively enforced in the great cities of New York, Chicago, Philadelphia, and Detroit (conveniently only a mile across the river from nonprohibitionist Canada). The 19th Amendment, mandating women's suffrage, led urban Democrats to fear that immigrant wives would defer to their husbands and not vote, while Protestant Republican women would vote in great numbers. That is effectively what happened (and what had happened in Illinois when it allowed women to vote in 1916) until the presidential nomination of the Catholic Democrat Al Smith in 1928.

Disillusion with big government and economic instability, fear of revolutionary upheaval, and bitterness over the aftermath of World War I resulted in a sharp turn against Wilson's party. In the 1920 election, the Republican, Warren Harding, defeated his Democratic opponent, James M. Cox, by a devastating 60 to 34 percent.

CHAPTER 6

The Republicans' Return, the Democrats' Wilderness Years

Harding's victory over Cox was more than a resurrection of the McKinley majorities that Republicans won between 1896 and 1908. Besides carrying every non-Confederate state except Kentucky, Harding won Tennessee, and carried the Germano-Scandinavian states and the New England states by wide margins. He won most rural and small-town counties outside the South, as well as the industrial big cities. Not even the South was solidly Democratic. Harding was competitive in the Upper South, winning 55 percent in West Virginia, 50 percent in Oklahoma, 51 percent in Tennessee, 49 percent in Kentucky, and 43 percent in North Carolina.

Republican dominance continued through the 1920s. The persistence of the sharp recession into 1921 allowed Democrats to make gains, but not win majorities, in the congressional elections of 1922. And Democrats did win some races for governor and senator in marginal states like New York and Ohio during the 1920s. But Harding and his Republican successors pursued popular policies. They reduced income tax rates so that only the very rich were paying. They established the Bureau of the Budget and reduced spending, and not just on the military. They hosted and negotiated an international agreement on naval spending, preventing the arms race that had led to world war. They abandoned the prosecution of war opponents; Warren Harding not only commuted Eugene Debs's sentence, but invited him to the White

House for a friendly chat. These policies calmed the body politic after the frenzy of the war, and the immediate postwar years produced an era of technological innovation and economic growth.

The Republican Party's progressive and farm-belt members wanted to maintain something like the wartime farm subsidies, and many Republicans supported increased payments to World War I veterans. Senator George Norris, a progressive from Nebraska, sought to retain government ownership of a wartime munitions plant in Muscle Shoals, Alabama. In 1924, some Republicans supported the Progressive Party candidacy of Senator Robert LaFollette, who carried his home state of Wisconsin and got more than 40 percent in North Dakota and Minnesota; he had significant support in some industrial cities (Pittsburgh, Cleveland, Toledo, San Francisco) but did poorly in others (Philadelphia, Buffalo, Detroit). The Republican incumbent, Calvin Coolidge, won with 54 percent nationally, while LaFollette's got 17 percent and the Democrat, John W. Davis, 29 percent.

Four years later, Herbert Hoover, the commerce secretary, beat Al Smith, governor of New York, by a 58 to 41 percent margin. Hoover ran behind Harding's and Coolidge's showings in large cities and factory towns, as the urbanite Catholic Smith brought out many new voters there. But Smith's Catholicism cost him many votes in the South—where Hoover carried not only the six Upper South states but also Florida and Texas—and in much of the small-town and rural Midwest.

The difference between the contours of support in these two elections was less a reflection of the issue differences between the laissez-faire Coolidge and the interventionist Hoover than of the fissures in the Democratic Party. From its beginnings in the 1830s to the twenty-first century, the Democratic Party has been a coalition of out-groups, people not seen by themselves or by others as typical Americans—white southerners and Catholic immigrants in the nineteenth century, blacks and gentry liberals in the twenty-first. In his first term, Woodrow Wilson welded together a successful government of southern appointees and progressive measures, but the Democrats' coalition fell apart after the disasters of his second term.

The Democratic National Convention of 1924 took 103 ballots to select a nominee for president. Al Smith led on several ballots, but never won the two-thirds required for the nomination since 1836—a measure designed to give each of the party's disparate constituencies an effective veto. But the party's competing constituencies distrusted each other more than they opposed the Republicans. While Democratic nominees in the three elections of the 1920s carried or came close to carrying states with a total of 262 electoral votes, just 8 short of a majority, none of them actually won more than 137 electoral votes.

In the wake of the 1928 election, one could have written the history of the Democratic Party as a story of continuous decline, from the dominance of the Jacksonian Democracy in the three antebellum decades, to rough parity with the new Republican Party in the three decades after the War Between the States (as white southerners liked to call it), to a distinct but not desperate minority status in the quarter century after 1896 and ending in a plunge to an arguably threatening minority-party status in the 1920s. The party's two presidents since the Civil War, Grover Cleveland and Woodrow Wilson, had left office utterly repudiated, in Cleveland's case by his party and in both cases by the larger electorate.

The Democrats had an additional problem: finding good candidates. Most of their well-known officeholders were either southerners or Catholics, and it was generally thought that neither a southerner nor a Catholic could win a presidential election—a perception that Al Smith's defeat only strengthened. As Herbert Hoover took the oath of office in March 1929, only a handful of prominent officeholders were northern Protestant Democrats. The newly elected governor of New York, Franklin Roosevelt, had a famous name but had been elected only by a narrow margin. The other prominent northern Protestants were from the small states of Colorado, Montana, South Dakota, and Utah, and the quasi-southern states of Maryland and Oklahoma. There were seventeen Democratic senators from outside the South, but two were Catholics (the Walshes of Massachusetts and Montana), four were from quasi-southern states (Kentucky, Maryland, Missouri, Oklahoma), and nine were from small states west of the Mississippi River. The two others were from the key political state of New York, but the elderly doctor Royal Copeland was never seriously considered as a presidential candidate, and Robert Wagner was ineligible, being an immigrant from Germany.

What came next almost everyone with the least acquaintance with American political history knows. The stock market crashed in October

1929 and unemployment started to rise. In the next six months, Hoover and the Republican Congress cut taxes and appropriated large sums for federal building projects and state highway construction. During the months that Congress remained out of session, from June 1930 to the new Congress's first regular session (under the antique calendar still being used) in December 1931, the economy worsened, with foreign banking crises and nations going off the gold standard, and Hoover's signing of the protectionist Smoot-Hawley tariff and his pleas that employers not cut wages. This was all a profound disappointment to a public remembering how Hoover had been the great food administrator in Belgium and Russia in the 1910s and the organizer of relief from the terrible Mississippi River flood in 1927. Democrats fell just short of winning Senate and House majorities in the 1930 elections, with gains concentrated in border and rural states where Smith's Catholicism had hurt Democrats in 1928. Special-election victories in Michigan and Texas in November 1931 gave Democrats a majority in the House.

Unemployment rose to about 25 percent; Hoover was just starting to develop modern unemployment statistics. Not allowing wages to fall resulted in lost jobs, in contrast to the 1920–21 recession, which was quickly over and was followed by massive growth. The 1920 Census had revealed that, for the first time, most Americans lived in urban areas (defined as incorporated cities or towns with populations of 2,500 or more!), and the move to the cities accelerated in the following decade. In previous downturns, most Americans could make do with what they produced on their farms. Now you had an enormous population who had grown up on farms—in the Midwest or in eastern or southern Europe—and had moved to fast-growing cities where they enjoyed a standard of living that most had never dreamed of. Then, with banks closing and jobs disappearing, people found that the pieces of paper they had depended on were suddenly worthless.

Yet there was no fear of violent revolution as there had been in the years just after World War I. The Socialist candidate, Norman Thomas, got just 2.2 percent of the vote in 1932, while the Communist, William Foster, got 0.3 percent. There was no public health calamity like the influenza epidemic of 1918. Nor was there any perceptible danger of America becoming involved in another war: Mussolini was seen by many liberals as an innovative reformer; Hitler did not take office until January 1933;

and Japan's conquest of Manchuria was not seen as America's concern when voters went to the polls in 1932.

CHAPTER 7

Democrats Ascend

Franklin Roosevelt's 57 to 40 percent victory over Herbert Hoover was the largest Democratic majority up to that time—slightly greater than his Republican cousin's victory in 1904, though slightly smaller than Harding's and Hoover's victories twelve and four years earlier. He ran ahead of other Democrats by uniform margins across the country, except in New York and New England, where politics was largely a struggle of Catholic Democrats versus Protestant Republicans. Democrats made huge gains in congressional elections, to a 310-117 majority, thanks to economic conditions, but also because 1932 was the first time House districts were reapportioned among the states in twenty years, and many states, unable to redistrict, elected entire slates of Democrats. This was the only election since 1896 that resulted in a House where the majority of members were newly elected. In such circumstances, Roosevelt was enabled to enact measures designed to stop the downward spiral, notably the National Industrial Recovery Act seeking to impose wage and price floors on some 700 separate industries. This proved to be popular but unworkable; Congress was about to let the law expire when the Supreme Court declared it unconstitutional.

In 1934, Democrats actually gained House seats and increased their majority to 319-103, the only off-year election between 1838 and 2002 in which the president's party gained House seats. This was attributed by New Deal historians to Roosevelt's economic redistribution policies—steeply progressive income taxes, Social Security, the pro-union Wagner Act—but those Second New Deal policies were not adopted or even seriously discussed before 1935. In my book *Our Country: The Shaping of America from Roosevelt to Reagan*, I showed that there were two countervailing trends in 1934: Democrats lost seats in small-town and rural districts where they had made unprecedented gains in the trough-of-the-Depression year of 1932, but gained seats in industrial and immigrant districts, many of which had been solidly Republican in the 1920s. These gains could not have come from Second New Deal policies nonexistent in 1934; they are more plausibly attributed to First New Deal policies, which restored a sense of order and stability in place of a dizzyingly downward spiral. And the Democrats' 1934 losses can plausibly be seen as opposition to policies of national regimentation, which deprived local communities of power and control over their own fate.

The same pattern is evident in a comparison of the 1932 and 1936 presidential results. Roosevelt's share of the vote increased 12 percent in industrial Pennsylvania, 10 percent in New Jersey, 8 percent in Ohio, 5 percent in New York, 4 percent in Michigan, as well as 9 percent in California and Washington. But it declined 10 percent in the Dakotas, 6 percent in Oklahoma and Nebraska. Within large states there were similar contrasts. Roosevelt gained robustly in New York City and Chicago and Detroit, but lost ground in Upstate New York, Downstate Illinois, and Outstate Michigan. Big industrial cities that had been voting Republican for most of the preceding forty years—New York, Philadelphia, Pittsburgh, Cleveland, Detroit, Chicago, St. Louis—gave him 60 to 73 percent of their votes. It was on this basis that the New Deal historians, looking at the statewide totals and ignoring the details of the off-year results, concluded that the Democrats had gained a national majority due to New Deal redistributionist policies. They did gain a majority, but not for that reason, and not one that lasted as long as many thought.

The redistributionist policies that historians credit for a long-lasting Democratic majority quickly became a political liability. Sit-down strikes that began in the last days of December 1936 succeeded in unionizing most workers at major auto and steel factories, but also stirred up a backlash, which resulted in Republican victories in Michigan, Ohio, and Pennsylvania in 1938. Democrats in Congress killed Roosevelt's Supreme

Court packing proposal in 1937. Roosevelt's last domestic reform, a minimum wage that conveniently did not cover black or white farm workers in the South, was legislated by 1938. In the off-year elections of 1938, Democrats lost eighty House seats, and there came into being—albeit without any coherent legislative program—an informal alliance of Republicans and southern Democrats who dominated the House and the Senate for twenty years. Political alignments in 1938 and 1939 were roiled by isolationists, even as Roosevelt, who had supported earlier neutrality acts, deftly secured their demise in the months between the Munich Pact and the outbreak of World War II. Polling in 1939 revealed that Democratic domestic policies were unpopular and that Democrats, including Roosevelt, were trailing potential Republican candidates. And both parties had difficulty finding other candidates—Republicans because they had so few prominent candidates after their defeats in the 1930s, Democrats because they had few candidates except putatively ineligible southerners and Catholics.

Overshadowing all this political uncertainty was the specter of war. Adolf Hitler made war on Poland in September 1939, and Britain and France then declared war. Having already absorbed Austria and Czechoslovakia and made a nonaggression pact with the Soviet Union, Hitler quickly overran Poland. He invaded Denmark and Norway in April 1940, then struck suddenly at France, Belgium, and the Netherlands in May, forcing France to surrender by mid-June. This was the closest the world has ever come to the vision of George Orwell's *1984*, with the totalitarians Hitler and Stalin controlling most of the landmass of Eurasia and threatening the Middle East, and their ally Japan controlling half of China and much of East Asia. Roosevelt, in the judgment of his shrewd biographer Conrad Black,[5] pursued a foreign policy aimed at the destruction of Hitler even as large majorities of Americans opposed involvement in the war. He was aided by the capture of the Republican nomination by Wendell Willkie, a businessman who until 1939 had been a Democrat and who shared his partiality toward embattled Britain. Roosevelt, having secured the Democratic nomination at a manipulated convention, took breathtaking steps to aid Britain: arranging for the transfer of destroyers, persuading Congress to authorize a military draft, and recruiting William Knudsen, the president of General Motors, to enlist the great manufacturing companies in initiating defense production. Having seen firsthand the shambles of government production in World War I, Roosevelt opted for the more efficient and flexible private sector: a surprising move, perhaps, for an economic redistributionist, and one that has set the template for the American defense industry ever since.

Turnout surged in the 1940 election, in dozens of counties to levels never again reached, and at higher levels than in the wartime and post-war elections of 1944 and 1948. Roosevelt was reelected to a third term by a 55 to 40 percent margin, but the contest was exceedingly close in the large Northeast and Midwest industrial states. All of Roosevelt's nearly five million popular-vote margin came from the South and the ten largest cities—New York, Chicago, Philadelphia, Detroit, Los Angeles, Cleveland, Baltimore, St. Louis, Boston, and Pittsburgh. In a counterfactual world with no Hitler and no World War II, it is unlikely that Roosevelt would have been nominated for a third term, and unlikely that he would have been elected if nominated. But in the world as it was, he won reelection in 1940 and again in 1944, when he had demonstrated his superb ability as commander in chief, and his successor, Harry Truman, won a full term in 1948, due in large (if unacknowledged) part to his successful leadership of a bipartisan foreign policy. This chain of events cemented in the minds of the public, and even more so in the analyses of academic historians, that the Democratic Party enjoyed natural majority support from the American public. I take a different view.

CHAPTER 8

A Natural Majority?

In the first half of the twentieth century, first the Democratic Party in 1920 and then the Republican Party in 1932 faced electoral disaster because of perceived and genuine failures, blunders, and bad luck. Contrary to the view of many historians, the Republican dominance in the 1920s was stronger and more fundamental than the Democratic dominance in the 1930s. Absent the Great Depression, Republican dominance would likely have continued, interspersed with occasional Democratic victories; absent World War II, the Democratic Party would have settled for something like rough parity with the Republicans— as Sean Trende argues persuasively that it did starting with Dwight Eisenhower's victory in 1952, the first election in which the GI generation participated in significant numbers.[6]

The larger point is that both parties, despite grave injury, managed not just to survive but to maintain sufficient vitality to thrive in the wake of electoral disaster. The specter of third-party competition, so lively at the beginning of the 1910s, did not revive after the disaster of the Democratic Party in 1920, much less after the Republican disaster of 1932. Almost every time one or the other party loses an election by a significant margin, or loses one unexpectedly as in 2016, there is speculation that it is on the verge of disappearance. The lesson of the first half of the twentieth century is that they both have shown the capacity to survive even the most dire political disasters.

II

The Parties in Our Times

CHAPTER 9

The Postwar Attempt to Produce Ideologically Polarized Politics

"We ought to have two real parties," Franklin Roosevelt told an aide in 1944, "one liberal and the other conservative."[7] It's a suggestion he shared with Wendell Willkie, his 1940 Republican opponent and then supporter of his policy of aiding Britain and his unofficial envoy in a round-the-world trip chronicled in his national bestseller, *One World*. Was this just idle chatter, halted by Willkie's unexpected death in October 1944 and Roosevelt's in April 1945? It is always difficult to distinguish Roosevelt's actual purposes from his blandishments and casual flatteries, but there is reason to believe he was serious in these speculations.

He was no stranger to the reshuffling of party loyalties: he was the vice presidential nominee on the Democratic ticket that won only 34 percent of the popular vote in 1920 and the presidential nominee on the Democratic tickets that won 57 and 61 percent of the popular vote in 1932 and 1936, with a coalition made up (as the anti–New Deal journalist Frank Kent wrote) of traditional anti-statist Democrats and pro-statist supporters of the 1924 Progressive Party candidate, Robert LaFollette. Roosevelt never expressed regret for his attempted purge of conservative Democrats in the 1938 primaries, even though all but one such effort failed. He treated the rejection of his redistributionist Second New Deal policies in the 1938 off-year elections and in polls in the 1940 election cycle as only a temporary setback. Instead, he rolled out proposals for increasing federal direction of the economy, something in the nature of a Third New Deal, in 1939 and 1940.[8]

More important, as World War II broke out in Europe, with the Soviet Union and Nazi Germany as allies and on the verge of gaining a stranglehold on the landmass of Eurasia, Roosevelt concentrated on foreign policy. And it was the international emergency rather than any economic policies that enabled Roosevelt to win an unprecedented third term in 1940, as polls made clear.

By the beginning of 1944, it was apparent that America and its Allies would win the war, and Roosevelt's mind turned to domestic policy—to expanding government and redistributing income. Perhaps he expected that the successful war effort would increase public confidence in the efficacy of government and centralized command and control. Perhaps he believed that the British wartime coalition's Beveridge Report, unveiled in December 1943, with its proposal for a massive postwar welfare state and nationalization of "commanding heights" industries, would appeal to Americans as well. Perhaps he assumed, as historians and political scientists have for years, that his redistributionist Second New Deal policies—steeply progressive taxes, encouragement of industrial labor unions, Social Security—accounted for the Democratic Party's victories in five consecutive presidential elections. But at least two of those victories, in 1940 and 1944, were due to foreign issues in a time of war and international peril. And enthusiasm for Second New Deal policies visibly waned as they were put in effect. Republicans gained eighty seats in the House of Representatives in the 1938 election, and for the next twenty years Congress was dominated almost uninterruptedly by a conservative coalition of Republicans and southern Democrats.

In any case, Roosevelt set out a radical platform in his January 1944 State of the Union address. There he argued that the "political rights" set forth in the Constitution, "our rights to life and liberty," may have been enough for the first century or so of the Republic, but were "inadequate" as "our industrial economy expanded." The interwar period showed, he said, that "people who are hungry and out of a job are the stuff of which dictatorships are made," and that "true individual freedom cannot exist without economic security." So he called for a "Second Bill of Rights," a set of entitlements that could only be provided by a much larger and more active government than he had taken charge of in 1933.

Roosevelt's policies would require a government financed by steeply progressive taxes, with power to control wages as well as crop and food prices, and to prevent strikes and "make available for war production or for any other essential services every able-bodied adult in the nation." This government would guarantee everyone jobs, education, clothing, housing, medical care, and financial security against the risks of old age and sickness.

A political realignment would be needed to achieve these goals, which were by no means unanimously supported by Democrats in the 1930s. Many Democrats, and not just in the South, considered themselves the ideological heirs of Thomas Jefferson, who abhorred a large centralized government and distrusted dwellers in crowded cities. Even Roosevelt portrayed himself as Jefferson's political heir and made a point of building the Jefferson Memorial, visible through the southern windows of the White House. And many self-styled southern Jeffersonians were Roosevelt's strongest supporters when he sought to build up the military and direct aid to Britain in the months before Pearl Harbor— which was opposed by many of the midwestern and western progressives who were the staunchest supporters of Roosevelt's economic policies. Similarly, southern Democrats opposed a modest antilynching bill, while the leading New Deal supporters of equal rights for blacks—Harold Ickes, Henry Wallace, Eleanor Roosevelt—were former Republicans. It would have been difficult in these years to find eligible recruits for a party that required members to take what were considered liberal (or conservative) stands on every major issue.

When Roosevelt died suddenly in April 1945, it was by no means clear that his successor, Harry Truman, would pursue his policies or partisan strategy. In his ten years as a senator he had a New Deal voting record, but this could simply have reflected the party loyalty of a politician who had been a steadfast member of the Prendergast machine in Kansas City. As president, Truman necessarily concentrated on foreign policy and saw the Democratic Party absorb historic losses in the 1946 off-year congressional elections. The question was whether to oppose the policies of the new coalition of Republicans and conservative Democrats: whether to move forward (as liberals saw it) to the Second Bill of Rights or backward to Jeffersonian libertarianism. Greatly influenced by a memorandum written by the New Deal lawyer James Rowe and transmitted by the presidential aide Clark Clifford, Truman decided to oppose the Republican 80th Congress root and branch, even as he worked with Republicans to develop the Cold War foreign policy—the Truman Doctrine, the Marshall Plan, NATO.

Much has been made of the differences between so-called liberal Republicans who tended to accept much of the New Deal and conservatives who sought to roll it back. But by 1945 they were united in opposition to the Second Bill of Rights. They took the case to the voters in the 1946 off-year elections with the slogan "Had enough?" The result was a Republican victory unmatched between 1928 and 2014: Republicans won the popular vote by a 54 to 45 percent margin and won 246 seats in the House to 188 for the Democrats. Moreover, 117 of these Democrats were from southern states. Even as this 80th Congress staunchly supported the Marshall Plan and the Truman administration's anti-Communist foreign policy, it repealed wage and price controls and lowered tax rates. Wartime restrictions that lasted into the 1950s in Britain suddenly disappeared in the United States.

Perhaps the most contentious issue in the immediate postwar years was the place of labor unions. They were greatly favored by the Wagner Act of 1935 and by wartime labor regulations, which led to the increase in union membership from 7 percent of the civilian workforce in 1933 to 27 percent in 1944, including most auto, steel, rubber, and defense workers. Once wartime regulations and agreements lapsed, strikes proliferated, and 1946 saw the second largest number of workdays lost to strikes in American history (after 1919, another postwar year). There was widespread agreement that the Wagner Act needed at least some changes, and Senator Robert Taft of Ohio, in a bravura legislative performance, fashioned a bill on the Senate floor. It defined unfair labor practices by unions, allowed the president to impose an eighty-day cooling-off period for strikes, prohibited political contribution of union dues, and banned Communists from union offices. Closed-shop contracts requiring all employees to join unions were permitted, but not in states prohibiting them with right-to-work laws—a bit of federalism which effectively blocked unionization in the South and the Great Plains. Truman, on the advice of James Rowe transmitted by Clark Clifford, took a stand congruent with Roosevelt's Second Bill of Rights and vetoed this Taft-Hartley Act. But his veto was overridden by wide margins in both houses of Congress. Union membership peaked at 28 percent of the civilian workforce in 1953–54, eventually falling below 10 percent of private sector workers in the 1990s.

There was similarly meager support for Truman's proposals for vast public housing programs and federal aid to education. The issue of civil rights for blacks was a different matter. Black Americans' military service and casualties in the war created a compelling argument for equal treatment afterward, one with a powerful impact on many white Americans including Harry Truman. It prompted him to back the creation of a civil rights commission and to order desegregation of the military (not immediately effective). Politically, these measures were an asset not so much with blacks (who mostly were not allowed to vote in the South and who had only started their massive movement to the North) as with Jewish voters, a key independent group in politically marginal megastates, particularly New York. And there was a downside risk. The civil rights plank in the Democratic National Convention's 1948 platform led to the walkout by Strom Thurmond, the governor of South Carolina, and to his campaign as a States' Rights Democrat in which he carried four hitherto heavily Democratic southern states with 38 electoral votes (plus one stray elector from Tennessee).

Another issue that would have been novel before the war was Truman's anti-Communist Cold War policy. The Marshall Plan for recovery in Western Europe, Truman's opposition to Soviet takeovers in Eastern Europe, and his staunch support of the Berlin airlift—ordered in July 1948 over the advice of military and foreign advisers—were popular among many Republicans and most Democrats. But Henry Wallace, Truman's predecessor as vice president and an opponent of his Cold War policies, ran his own campaign under the Progressive label and won more than one million popular votes, over a third of them from the five boroughs of New York City.

Even with these southern and leftist defections, Truman won the popular vote by a 50 to 45 percent margin and Democrats regained significant margins in both houses of Congress. But this result did not prove to be the wave of the future. Truman's charges that Republicans would cut farm subsidies helped him carry midwestern and western states whose isolationism kept them out of the Democratic column in 1940 and 1944. But the farm population was in the midst of a steep decline, from 25 percent of the nation in the 1930s to under 5 percent in the late 1950s. Moreover, voter turnout dropped from 49.9 million in 1940 to 48.8 million in 1948. The GI generation, highly supportive of FDR during the war but largely blocked from voting absentee by congressional Republicans and southern Democrats, had not really joined the electorate and would not be a major force until 1952, when turnout increased to 61.8 million.

Nor did Democrats' recapture of congressional majorities result in passage of anything like Roosevelt's Second Bill of Rights. Proposals to build on New Deal housing programs, to make the federal government the chief provider of new housing, were rejected. So-called urban renewal programs, involving slum clearance and high-rise construction, took so long to implement as to have little impact on housing supply; only in New York City were a substantial share of new housing units built by government. Government ownership or superintendence of private firms, an implied goal if government was to guarantee jobs for everyone, was not contemplated; indeed, Roosevelt had declined to nationalize railroads and shipyards as he had seen the Wilson administration do when he was part of it during World War I. Federal aid to education, whipsawed between big-city Democrats who demanded support for Catholic schools and southern Democrats who opposed it, did not pass Congress until 1965. Harry Truman's plan for something like the British National Health Service was rejected, and only partially realized in 1965 with the passage of Medicare (for the elderly) and Medicaid (for the indigent). Social Security old-age pensions were spared from attack, and the amazingly long-lived architects of that 1935 act successfully promoted extensions, including disability payments, in the 1950s and early 1960s.

To a surprising degree, American public policy was already in place. A choice was made to reject Roosevelt's Second Bill of Rights in favor of free enterprise tempered by high taxation and varieties of regulation, with government absorbing less of the economy and acting as less of a guiding force than in contemporary Western Europe or fast-growing Japan. This domestic policy proved to be enduring for a half century or more, though significantly modified by the 1965 Great Society legislation. The Social Security safety net was expanded, quietly at first in the 1950s with increases in benefits and the creation of disability benefits, and more visibly with the creation of Medicare and Medicaid by the Democratic supermajorities elected in 1964 in the wake of John Kennedy's assassination. The Cold War policy established by the Truman administration and Republicans led by Arthur Vandenberg, the previously isolationist chairman of the Senate Foreign Relations Committee, endured with solid bipartisan support for two decades, and despite significant dovish opposition in the two decades that followed John Kennedy's and Lyndon Johnson's decision to go to war in Vietnam.

This is not a picture of a nation moving resolutely left to become a predominantly Democratic country, which was something between fantasy and partisan exaggeration. It was stated most persuasively in 1952 by the journalist Samuel Lubell's often insightful book *The Future of American Politics*, which depicted the Democratic Party as the natural majority party, having won its fifth consecutive presidential election in 1948 despite the separate Thurmond and Wallace candidacies. But Republicans had also won a solid political victory in 1946, followed by far more success in enacting their policies than the Democrats would have in enacting theirs. And that fifth consecutive Democratic presidential victory in 1948 was followed four years later with a much larger victory, among a much expanded electorate, for the Republican, Dwight Eisenhower. These years were the beginning of a political era when the GI generation was a predominant force and one in which, contrary to conventional wisdom, the Democratic Party did not enjoy a natural majority.

It was also a nation in which voting behavior was rooted in history, determined by traumatic events long past but not at all forgotten. Parts of the postwar nation had an economics-based, management-versus-labor politics, most notably in the industrial belt, including my home city of Detroit, where the 1930s organizing of the industrial unions was still controversial decades later. In the great metropolitan areas of the Northeast, the political divide reflected ethnic and religious divisions. Black voters, heavily Republican until the 1930s, were mostly Democratic though a swing group over the next three decades. Barred from voting in most of the South by devices like poll taxes and literacy tests but most of all by blatant discrimination until the Voting Rights Act of 1965, they started voting near-unanimously Democratic in 1964. White southerners, heavily Democratic in the 1930s and 1940s, were increasingly split between affluent Republicans in the rising cities and stubborn Democrats in small towns. It is often said that Republicans gained strength in the South only after their nominee Barry Goldwater opposed the Civil Rights Act of 1964. But in fact Republican presidential nominees won 49 percent of the popular vote in the South in 1952, 50 percent in 1956, and 48 percent in 1960—and a significantly lower 47 percent, the lowest since the 1940s, in 1964.

All in all, Americans in this postwar politics were roughly equally divided between the two parties, with Republicans holding an advantage, widening in the late 1960s, in presidential elections, and Democrats holding an advantage, widening about the same time, in congressional and state elections. In the ten presidential elections from 1952 to 1988, Republicans averaged 52 percent of the popular vote (and 367 electoral votes), while Democrats averaged 45 percent (and 163 electoral votes). But political commentators almost to the very end of this period still referred to Democrats as the natural majority party, in part because Democrats maintained majorities in both houses of Congress between 1932 and 1994. In those 62 years, Republicans held majorities in the Senate only after the elections of 1946, 1952, 1980, 1982, and 1984, and majorities in the House only after the elections of 1946 and 1952. They received 49 percent of the popular vote for House of Representatives in 1950, 1952, and 1956, but the closest they came to that mark again before their breakthrough in 1984 was the 48 percent they won in 1966, 1968, and 1980.

This unprecedented—and now abandoned—rate of ticket splitting was the result of three factors. The first is that even as Republicans were routinely winning about 50 percent of the presidential vote in the South—Dwight Eisenhower was the first to do this, as early as 1952— virtually no Republicans were elected to Congress from southern states or districts for three decades. The only exceptions up through the late 1970s were in mountain areas that opposed secession in the Civil War— in Virginia, West Virginia, and Kentucky—and among upscale voters, some of northern origins, in fast-growing urban areas—Arlington, Virginia (outside Washington); Charlotte, North Carolina; Tampa–St. Petersburg; Dallas. For many years the only Republican senator from a former Confederate state was John Tower of Texas, first elected in 1961 to fill the vacancy caused by Lyndon Johnson's election as vice president, when liberals supported him to oppose his very conservative

Democratic opponent on the theory that he could easily be beaten by a more liberal Democrat in the next election. (Instead, he was reelected three times and retired in 1984.)

The second factor is that the rough balance between the parties was obscured by wide oscillations in party percentages in the ten presidential contests from 1952 to 1988. This made it easy to imagine these must reflect massive changes in party identification, and much political commentary was about whether the Republican Party would disappear after Barry Goldwater's loss or the Democratic Party after George McGovern's. But the landslide reelections overstate the underlying partisan fluctuations. What seems to have been happening is that voters with vivid memories of the Depression of the 1930s and the Second World War of the 1940s chose to reward incumbent presidents of both parties who seemed to produce prosperity and peace by reelecting them with supermajorities: 57 percent for Dwight Eisenhower in 1956; 61 percent in 1964 for Lyndon Johnson, the legatee for the assassinated John Kennedy, who was on his way to winning almost as great a supermajority according to polling in 1963; 61 percent for Richard Nixon in 1972; 59 percent for Ronald Reagan in 1984. The fact that three of these four presidents were Republicans accounts for most of that party's edge in average percentage of the vote over that period. Three of the four presidential elections in which no previously elected incumbent was on the ballot—1960, 1968, 1976—were almost equally divided.

The third factor is that party support varied in different regions, rooted in different historical experiences. A map of the partisan preferences in this era might look like a Renaissance painter's palimpsest, with one layer of pigment obscuring but not entirely erasing an earlier one. Traces of Civil War preferences remained on the landscape, especially in hard-fought Appalachian battlegrounds and in the Georgia counties through which General Sherman's troops marched to the sea. Clashes between Yankee Protestants, who began arriving in the 1620s, and Irish Catholics, who began arriving in the 1840s, were imprinted seemingly indelibly in the political map of New England and in the big industrial metropolises of the Northeast and the Midwest. Roman Catholics, concentrated in large northern metropolitan areas, voted heavily for John Kennedy in 1960 and for Lyndon Johnson four years later, only to be roughly evenly divided between the parties starting in 1968. The pacifist-minded German and Scandinavian immigrants in the late nine-teenth century made the Upper Midwest the most pacifist/isolationist/dovish region of the nation. The labor strife and sit-down strikes of the 1930s made the industrial belt from Pennsylvania west to Illinois the scene of class-warfare politics between supporters of management and unions.

This political palimpsest was inherently unstable, as events that once swayed political choices were obscured by the emergence of other issues or just the passage of time. Both political parties, having survived devastating electoral setbacks in the century, hustled to adapt to circumstance. Both succeeded, and thus managed to maintain something like parity in presidential elections in the three postwar decades. The winning candidates and parties in the close presidential elections of 1948, 1960, 1968, and 1976 succeeded by gaining extra votes among identifiable segments of the electorate that had supported the other party in recent elections. Harry Truman succeeded in 1948 by carrying farm-belt voters whose isolationism had led them to vote against Franklin Roosevelt in 1940 and 1944. John Kennedy won with an overwhelming 78 percent (according to Gallup) among Catholics, netting him more electoral votes than he lost due to his relatively low 37 percent among white Protestants. (And as the political scientist Sean Trende has noted, there is a serious case that Kennedy didn't win the popular vote.)[9] Richard Nixon won in 1968 by running far better in suburbs and the outer neighborhoods of large metro areas, especially but not entirely among Catholics, than he had eight years before. And Jimmy Carter won in 1976 by running better than any nonincumbent Democrat since 1945 among southern white evangelicals and southern-accented small-town and rural voters in close states like Ohio and Missouri.

CHAPTER 10

How the Republican Party Sloughed Off Its Liberals

Franklin Roosevelt's wartime suggestion—invitation—to Wendell Willkie to work together to create one clearly liberal party did not come to fruition during the few years left to them, nor for at least another half century. But it did attract attention and was taken up by E. E. Schattschneider and dozens of other political scientists. The public was polled on it repeatedly by George Gallup, and it was given favorable coverage in the *New York Times* and the *Washington Post*.

The idea appealed especially to liberals, supporters of something like Roosevelt's Second Bill of Rights, who assumed that one party would usually control the White House and both houses of Congress (as parties had in 44 of the 50 years between 1896 and 1946) and that this party would usually be the liberal party—which could presumably steamroller its program through as expeditiously as Clement Attlee's Labour Party had in postwar Britain. American political history over the next 70 years can be seen as a story of how these midcentury political scientists' prayers were largely but only partially answered, how the Democratic Party became uniformly liberal and the Republican Party uniformly conservative, much to the consternation of twenty-first-century political scientists and editorial writers.

This process did not happen by design, nor by conspiracy; it was the work of many political actors, including voters. I see it as the result of the workings of the political marketplace in a period of continuing sharp competition between two long-established political parties to win over an electorate for whom historically rooted political allegiances and attitudes were in the process of becoming less relevant and in which news media with near-monopoly reach—three television networks, heavily influenced by the *New York Times* and the *Washington Post*—had not yet squandered their reputation for objectivity and fairness. I have described this process in political narrative in my 1990 book, *Our Country: The Shaping of America from Roosevelt to Reagan.*

Another way to examine it is to try to answer two questions. The first is: Why did liberal Republicans stay Republican, and when and why did they stop doing so? The second is: Why did conservative Democrats stay Democratic, and when and why did they stop doing so?

So what was keeping liberal Republicans Republican? The quick answer is that they were motivated, as politicians and voters so often area—and not just in our own era, as some like to think—more by those whose beliefs and behavior they disliked than by those whom they admired. Midcentury liberal Republicans disliked the Democrats identified by Theodore H. White in *The Making of the President 1960* as the three types of politicians who were the dominant forces in any Democratic National Convention: big-city machine bosses, segregationist southern officeholders, and aggressive labor union leaders.[10] The first two, or their equivalents, had been major powers in the party since before the Civil War, while the industrial union leaders zoomed suddenly to national prominence in the 1930s. At the end of World War II, Republicans—politicians and voters—had spent most of their adult lives in a country where the Republican Party had enjoyed majority support and governmental responsibilities in most of the nation most of the time. It was the default party of investment bankers and corporate executives, of factory workers and farmers, of small-town businessmen and traveling salesmen, in the Northeast and Midwest and West and even for many in the Upper South. Men with experience in government and the law were mostly Republicans. It seemed to be the natural ruling party, and for most of the half century before 1945 it was.

This ruling class and the millions of Republican voters who largely shared its views regarded the urban bosses, southern segregationists, and industrial union leaders as menaces to the nation. From the days of the antebellum New York Whig diarists Philip Hone and George

Templeton Strong until the 1950s congressional hearings featuring the New York Democrat Frank Costello, the Democratic machines were regarded as interlinked with organized crime and violence. Big-city machines were seen as corruptly inflating the cost of government and falsifying election returns (although one should note that there were governing Republican machines too, most notably in Philadelphia). Segregationist southern Democrats were looked at with disfavor as betrayers of Republican-led success in the Civil War and in passing the Reconstruction constitutional amendments, and as impediments to industrial development and economic growth. Some Republicans at least occasionally tried to advance equal rights for blacks out of strong personal conviction—including Henry Cabot Lodge, Warren G. Harding, Arthur Vandenberg, and Thomas Dewey. And for Republicans who respected and admired the leaders of the large industrial corporations, impressed by their willingness to make huge and risky capital investments and technological innovations, the industrial unions were lawless and violent predators. The sit-down strikes of 1936–39 are sentimentally remembered now in Flint and Akron, but were blatantly illegal—then and now—seizures of property, which achieved their goal of union representation only because Democratic governors (defeated in the next elections) refused to enforce the law. Many Republicans, including leaders of the major auto, steel, and rubber companies, were favorably impressed by the unions' cooperation in the wartime industrial effort and willingly or grudgingly accepted them as postwar permanent institutions, while still regarding them as unwelcome deviations from the natural order of things.

Republicans entered postwar politics by winning large congressional majorities but were unable to retain them, with the exception of the two years following Dwight Eisenhower's victory in 1952. One reason was the policy successes of the 80th Congress in 1947 and 1948, which Democratic majorities were unable to significantly reverse in multiple succeeding Congresses. Nothing can be so fatal for a political party as the enduring success of your signature public policy initiatives: voters then turn to other issues on which your opponents may have the edge. In addition, Republicans made a disabling strategic error by continuing to resist the principle of equal-population congressional and legislative districts.

Republican-controlled Congresses, in defiance of the Constitution's command, had refused to reapportion House seats among the states in accordance with the 1920 Census. This refusal was a response to the Census Bureau's announcement that most Americans now lived in what it defined as urban areas. As commerce secretary and as president, Herbert Hoover championed a bill that would require automatic reapportionment of 435 seats, by applying an arithmetical formula to Census results. Senator Arthur Vandenberg of Michigan, with the largest population percentage gain of any significant-sized state in that decade, insisted on an amendment removing the requirement, first established in 1842, for equal-population districts; he did not want booming and potentially Democratic Detroit to get new districts at the expense of slow-growing, safely Republican Outstate Michigan.[11]

Vandenberg's compromise, embedded in the Reapportionment Act of 1929, was little noticed but hugely influential in the postwar years. It tended to guarantee that Republicans from rural and small-town districts with stagnant populations would control state legislatures, which in turn would create congressional district plans, or leave in place old ones that heavily overrepresented rural areas and small areas of central cities once thronged with recent immigrants. Most heavily underrepresented was booming postwar America: neighborhoods at the edges of central cities—Queens and the outer reaches of Brooklyn and the Bronx in New York City, far northwest and southwest Chicago, northeast Philadelphia, northwest Detroit—and adjacent suburbs. These areas also tended to be politically marginal, the swing districts that determined whether the big swing states with their multiple electoral votes—New York, New Jersey, Pennsylvania, Ohio, Michigan, Illinois—would go Democratic or Republican. They voted Republican in 1946, but in the years that followed, especially the 1954 and 1958 off-year elections, they voted increasingly Democratic, often for young liberal candidates with no ties to urban machines (but in many cases to industrial labor unions).

In effect, these areas were the training camps for the development of talented political players, used effectively by Democrats and much less so by Republicans. Republicans could still win majorities of seats in some large states so long as district lines in population-stagnant areas stayed in place. But they were failing to develop major-league talent that could prevail in statewide elections in competitive states. And when the Supreme Court required equal-population districts in 1964, the Republican advantage in House and state legislative seats largely vanished.

Not all Republicans were unaware of the need to carry these fast-growing areas. These were, by and large, not in the midwestern and northeastern small towns and rural counties that produced most Republican congressmen and legislators, but in the nation's largest metropolitan areas (none of which in 1945 were in the South). They tended to be in large states with many electoral votes—states that were conspicuously marginal in the three presidential elections of the 1940s. In seven states with a total of 157 to 160 electoral votes, the margin in all three elections was less than 5 percent; and in Pennsylvania, with 35 electoral votes, that was the case in two of the three elections. These states included Illinois, Iowa, Michigan, Ohio, and Wisconsin in the Midwest, and New York and New Jersey in the Northeast.

New York was of particular importance, being the nation's most populous state, with 47 electoral votes, as well as the world's greatest financial and media center. This was the home of a highly competent and self-confident Republican elite: investment bankers and corporate executives and media moguls whose offices were concentrated around Wall Street and the Midtown blocks lined with men's clubs around Grand Central Station. Their most visible and articulate spokesman was Henry Luce, founder of *Time, Life,* and *Fortune.* The editor of *Fortune,* Russell Davenport, was given time off to run Wendell Willkie's successful campaign for the 1940 Republican nomination, and Luce's publications promoted the political rise of Thomas Dewey from Manhattan district attorney to governor of New York and then to the Republican presidential nominee in 1944 and 1948.

These eastern establishment Republicans favored an internationalist foreign policy abroad and acceptance or accommodation of many (not all) New Deal programs at home. Electorally their instinct was to cultivate enough big-city votes to remain competitive in statewide and therefore in national elections. Their paradigmatic model, of course, was New York State, whose electorate was closely split between Catholic City Democrats and Protestant Upstate Republicans. Jewish voters, with 15 percent of the vote, held the balance, but were not centrist: they were suspicious of both major parties and were more liberal than either party's base on both economic and cultural issues. New York Republicans had been courting these voters at least since Theodore Roosevelt appointed the first Jewish cabinet member in 1904, and these efforts continued under Dewey and with Senators Irving Ives and Jacob Javits, who were among the nation's foremost postwar opponents of discrimination against blacks and Jews. In their quest for what Samuel Lubell called the "urban vote"—a euphemism for Jews and some gentile liberals with similar views—they stressed their general acceptance of New Deal policies and their opposition to corrupt big-city Democratic machines and muscle-bound labor unions. This was a successful strategy: Republicans held New York's governorship for all but four of the 32 years between 1942 and 1974, and carried or came within 5 percent of carrying New York in all but one presidential election in that span.

The other large marginal states in the early postwar years, though not identical to New York, had similar characteristics (with the obvious exception of Iowa). Each had smaller but not insignificant proportions of Jewish voters and a similar ethnic and racial mix. Each tended to be divided between one very large metropolitan area with an urban Democratic political machine, a suburban ring that enjoyed some of the nation's fastest population growth in the first two postwar decades, and a large swathe of rural and small-town counties of Republican heritage. Each had major manufacturing industries and a labor union movement that had grown much stronger in the 1930s. Each tended to have a partisan division close to the nation's: New York's Republican and Democratic percentages in elections from 1856 to 1960 seldom varied more than 5 percent from the national average, and were often much closer.[12]

So the liberal Republican strategy was to stay close to Democrats on substantive issues while remaining harshly critical of their reliance on big-city political machines and sometimes violent labor unions and their allies in organized crime, and to criticize northern Democrats for their frequent collusion in Congress with southern Democrats blocking civil rights legislation. Unsuccessful in the presidential elections of the 1940s, this strategy was hugely successful in the 1950s thanks to the sterling qualifications of Dwight Eisenhower, whose policy views were congruent with it, and it gained Richard Nixon, another believer who always feared the economic appeal of big-government policies, almost exactly the same number of votes as his opponents in 1960 and 1968. Gerald Ford in 1976 nearly equaled Jimmy Carter's vote count despite the handicap of running as the appointed (and Senate-confirmed) successor after Richard Nixon was forced to resign in disgrace.

By this time most of the liberal Republicans had become Democrats. One defining moment came in 1968. The task of filling the Senate vacancy caused by the murder of Robert Kennedy fell to Nelson Rockefeller, governor of New York, a liberal Republican certainly as a big spender (it was said that he spent the public's money as if it were his own) and on cultural issues (he signed a 1968 bill largely legalizing abortion) though not in foreign policy (he was a staunch backer of the Vietnam War and of his protégé Henry Kissinger). Rockefeller offered the seat to his nephew Jay Rockefeller, who with his massive financial resources might have held it for life. But the younger Rockefeller, already elected secretary of state in West Virginia as a Democrat, wanted no identification with his uncle's party and turned the offer down. He was elected governor of West Virginia and then a U.S. senator, serving as a staunch Democrat from 1976 to 2014.

The reason for the decline—the virtual disappearance—of liberal Republicans was the fact that the repugnant features of the Democratic Party largely disappeared. The power of big-city urban machine bosses was disappearing, as civil service replaced patronage jobs and later as public employee unions, in effect financed by tax money, gained increasing clout. In addition, the movement of white ethnics to the suburbs and the in-migration of hundreds of thousands of southern blacks—developments in train between 1940 and 1965 robbed the bosses of their most sympathetic constituencies. Richard J. Daley, mayor of Chicago and the dominant machine boss at the 1968 Democratic National Convention, was denied a seat at the convention four years later at the behest of a delegation including academic liberals and Jesse Jackson. He was seated in 1976, but his power was diminished. He died in December that year, a month after the election of Jimmy Carter.

The second pillar of the Democratic Party as it entered the 1960s, the conservative southern governors, became either less conservative or clearly separated from the national party. Alabama's George Wallace took the latter course, running a loud but unavailing primary challenge of Lyndon Johnson in 1964, launching a third-party candidacy that won

14 percent of national votes and 46 electoral votes in 1968, then running again for the Democratic nomination in 1972 and 1976. Wallace backed away from his "segregation forever" 1960s platform after passage of the Voting Rights Act of 1965 effectively enfranchised southern blacks. Other southern politicians did likewise, and there was no significant discernible constituency for segregation by the end of the decade. Other Democrats moved to the Republican Party, notably John Connally, the Texas governor who led the forces loyal to Lyndon Johnson at the 1968 Democratic National Convention and by February 1971 was appointed treasury secretary by Richard Nixon, for whom he cut "Democrats for Nixon" campaign ads in 1972.

The third Democratic constituency group obnoxious to liberal Republicans, the leadership of the big industrial labor unions, was a declining force in American economic and political life by the 1970s. Union membership peaked in 1954 at 35 percent of the private sector workforce. The power of unions had passed its peak as well: the United Mine Workers' bargaining leverage vanished as home heating shifted from coal to oil and natural gas; the power of the Teamsters Union vanished as the Kennedys' drive to prosecute its presidents Dave Beck and Jimmy Hoffa succeeded; the great industrial unions were not able to shut down big industries after their strikes against U.S. Steel in 1959 and General Motors in 1970. By 1971, leaders of the building trades unions and the AFL-CIO president George Meany were making clear their support of Richard Nixon's foreign policy and, in some cases, of his 1972 reelection campaign as well.

The fading out of the bêtes noires—the bosses, the segregationists, the unions—made the Democratic Party seem more palatable to many relatively affluent and highly educated voters—or their offspring—who had considered themselves Republicans in the past. And the increasing prominence of conservative politicians whose rhetoric suggested at least some rolling back of the New Deal—Barry Goldwater, Ronald Reagan— made the Republican label less attractive to some of these voters. As a consequence, New York ceased to be the fulcrum of presidential politics. The state voted 5 percent more Democratic than the rest of the nation in 1960 and 1968. By that decade its large number of Jewish voters were no longer repelled by the Democratic Party bosses, whose power was under attack by so-called "reform Democrats" and clearly in decline. In 1963,

Carmine De Sapio, the head of Tammany Hall in the 1950s, was defeated for district leader in his Greenwich Village home turf by a young lawyer named Edward Koch. Jewish voters, a group almost entirely overlapping with Samuel Lubell's "urban voters," were becoming solid Democratic voters and were unwilling to split their tickets in favor of just about any Republican, with the exception of Ronald Reagan (originally a liberal New Deal supporter himself). And the dwindling population of New York—the state lost nearly one million people in the 1970s—meant that its number of electoral votes declined from 47 in the elections of the 1930s and 1940s to 36 in 1984 and 1988.

CHAPTER 11

How the Democratic Party
Sloughed Off Its Conservatives

Why did conservative Democrats remain Democrats so long—and why and when did they stop supporting their ancestral party? For their first hundred years, the Democrats were the party of a smaller and less powerful federal government. They opposed federal public works, high tariffs, and enforcement of blacks' civil rights. They favored toleration of local institutions that many Republicans deemed abhorrent—slavery and segregation in the South, the saloons in the North. The progressive economic policies of the first two twentieth-century Democratic presidents, Woodrow Wilson and Franklin Roosevelt, were in tension with this Jeffersonian tradition, but not entirely at odds with it: Wilson's Federal Reserve had regional branches, and Roosevelt's minimum wage did not apply to most southern blacks. Roosevelt's Second Bill of Rights, a sharp departure from this tradition, was opposed by most southern Democratic politicians and given only lip service by most in the North. It was unclear in April 1945 whether Harry Truman would support such policies, and it remained so until he started opposing the Republican Congress in spring 1947—even as he was working cooperatively with it on foreign policy.

Nor were subsequent Democratic leaders clear supporters of what came to be known as liberal policies. Adlai Stevenson was anything but an enthusiast for civil rights. John Kennedy's initial priorities were free trade and increased defense spending. Lyndon Johnson's record from his first election victory in Texas in 1937 was speckled with ambiguity. Even after their big off-year victory in 1958, Democrats did not have clear congressional majorities who were sincere adherents of the dominant view. As majority leader in the Senate, Johnson was more interested in pursuing issue-specific coalitions across party lines, and his successor Mike Mansfield was not interested in pressing colleagues to vote his way. In the House, the longtime Speaker Sam Rayburn (first elected in 1912) was almost pathologically reluctant to challenge the sway of conservative committee chairmen, who were insulated from accountability to their caucus (more than at any other time in history) by the seniority system, and his successor, John McCormack (first elected in 1924/25), was similarly inert.[13] The effective leadership for liberal House Democrats came from AFL-CIO lobbyists and from the small Democratic Study Group organized in 1959 by junior Democrats like Eugene McCarthy.

"We have lost the South for a generation," Lyndon Johnson supposedly said after signing the Civil Rights Act of 1964.[14] But in presidential elections the South had not been heavily Democratic for more than a dozen years: Dwight Eisenhower and Richard Nixon, who had actively supported civil rights legislation, won 48 to 50 percent of southern votes in 1952, 1956, and 1960. Barry Goldwater, who voted against the Civil Rights Act (though he had integrated his Phoenix department store and the Arizona Air National Guard years before) would fall below that mark in November 1964, with 46 percent. And Richard Nixon, whose administration effectively integrated southern schools and initiated racial quotas and preferences, won a near-majority of southern electoral votes in a three-way race in 1968 and 69 percent of southern votes against George McGovern in 1972. The South would again vote for a Democratic nominee in 1976, when the party nominated Jimmy Carter of south Georgia in 1976. But not in the three previous presidential elections, and never again after 1980 except for the narrowest plurality in 1996. Starting in the 1980s, the South has always voted more Republican than the rest of the country in presidential contests, and in 1990 it began doing so in elections for the House of Representatives as well.

The key here was not Goldwater's vote against the Civil Rights Act, nor was there any hint that Republican candidates were more sympathetic than Democrats to legally enforced racial segregation. The key was foreign policy. For precisely half a century, from 1917 to 1967, the Democrats had been the party more supportive of military action overseas and robust defense budgets at home. Republicans supplied most of the votes against entry into World War I and for isolationist measures in the 1930s. Democratic presidents insisted on unconditional surrender in World War II and forged the anti-Communist Cold War postwar policy, with significant Republican support. In the 1960 presidential election it was the Democrat, John Kennedy, who called for more defense spending and more assertive action against Castro's Cuba, while the Republican, Richard Nixon, called for caution. One reason was that southern Democratic voters, and southern Democratic politicians, were the most hawkish identifiable voting bloc in all those years. Despite private reservations, they rallied to support John Kennedy's and Lyndon Johnson's increase of American troops from 15,000 to 550,000 in South Vietnam. With only a few exceptions, they continued to do so even as northern Democrats like Robert Kennedy and Eugene McCarthy called for de-escalation or abandonment of the Vietnam effort in 1967 and 1968. McCarthy's success in knocking Johnson out of the race in the New Hampshire primary, both candidates' successes in subsequent primaries and some caucuses, and their supporters' protests at the party's national convention in Chicago—and their success in passing, over Johnson's opposition, a resolution setting up a commission (headed by McGovern, as it turned out) to reform party nomination rules—made the Democratic Party appear dovish.

In contrast, Nixon and Republicans generally called for perseverance and for seeking something resembling victory in Vietnam. That contrast became more vivid once Nixon took office. Even though he ordered massive reductions in troops and de-escalation of the war, most non-southern and some southern Democrats who had supported without demur Johnson's escalation now called Nixon a warmonger and opposed what they called "Nixon's war." Democrats who took this approach had electoral success in many northern states, but not in the South. McGovern received only 29 percent of the popular vote in the South, carrying only two of 127 congressional districts there (a black majority district in Houston and a Hispanic majority district in San Antonio). Jimmy Carter, who navigated adeptly over the chasm between hawkishness and dovishness in the 1976 primaries, carried the South by a 54 to 45 percent margin. But after conducting an arguably dovish foreign policy—emphasizing pursuit of arms-control agreements with the Soviet Union that clearly lacked the votes needed for Senate ratification—he lost the South to Ronald Reagan in 1980, by 1.7 million votes, 52 to 44 percent.

From 1967 on through 1980, white southerners, tugged one way by ancestral loyalty to the Democratic Party and the other by their increasing disagreements with dominant Democratic politicians, became a moveable demographic group in presidential elections, replacing New York and large northern states resembling it as key target groups for both parties in the Electoral College in the late 1970s. Without his success in holding George Wallace to 46 electoral votes in the House, Richard Nixon would not have been elected president in 1968, just as Jimmy Carter would not have been elected in 1976 without the great bulk of southern electoral votes. The swing of all or almost all southern states to Republicans gave them huge Electoral College landslides in 1972 and 1980. White southerners, whose favored candidates lost most presidential elections from the 1860s to the 1960s, favored the winners in every election from 1968 to 1988. But just as New York ceased to be pivotal once it became a safe Democratic state by 1968, so the South ceased to be pivotal when in time it became safely Republican.

In 1960, for the third time in a row, about half of southern voters were voting Republican for president, and many more would do so in the next three elections, but the proportion voting Republican for House of Representatives was still far below 50 percent. In the general election, Republicans won just 9 of 126 seats, while Democrats won 63 seats unopposed. Why did the South continue to elect mostly Democrats to lower offices even as they mostly voted Republican for president? One reason was residual aversion to the Republican label dating to the Civil War. John Kennedy won his second highest statewide percentage in Georgia, because it was only 96 years after Sherman's troops had marched through. A second reason was that the national prominence of the political careers of George Wallace and Jimmy Carter provided southern politicians with templates for being a Democrat clearly different from those of the national leaders of the party.

Perhaps the most important reason for the lag in the Republican trend in congressional voting was that in much of the South in any given year there were simply no Republicans on the ballot. Aspiring politicians, whatever their views on issues, ran as Democrats because it was for many decades the only avenue to a political career. Virtually all southern state legislators and all but a handful of southern congressmen were Democrats, and those inclined to switch parties had to face the fact that all or most committee chairmen in state capitals and in Washington were Democrats.

When congressional Democrats changed their caucus rules after the influx of mostly young and antiwar liberals in the Watergate year of 1974,[15] House leaders were aware that they would not indefinitely have a 295-140 advantage and might lose their majority altogether without southern members, so they were careful to allow southerners from conservative districts to cast dissident votes on substantive issues so long as they voted for the leadership's "rules"—the terms and conditions on which bills could go to the floor—which usually guaranteed passage of what the leadership wanted. Democratic members who spurned this course would never be elected by the caucus to a committee or major subcommittee chairmanship, and indeed could be expelled from committees. This is what happened to the Texas Democrats Phil Gramm and Kent Hance when they cosponsored the Reagan tax and budget cuts in 1981. (Both then switched parties and were elected to other offices as Republicans.) Among politicians, conservative Democrats became almost extinct in the 1980s, and among voters they became largely absent from Democratic primary electorates by 2008.

The extinction of liberal Republicans and conservative Democrats was not apparent on the surface in the 1976 election, when the incumbent, Gerald Ford, defeated Ronald Reagan for the Republican nomination and Jimmy Carter defeated half a dozen more liberal opponents for the Democratic nomination. Both were from their parties' Civil War era heartlands: Ford from Outstate Michigan, Carter from south Georgia. But the weaknesses of their positions in their parties were apparent. Ford only narrowly defeated Reagan, and preemptively dropped his vice president, Nelson Rockefeller, the symbol of liberal Republicanism, in November 1975. Carter's nomination was also tenuous and he was regarded with suspicion by many liberal Democrats.

It has been noted that voting in the 1976 election was not geographically polarized: many more counties were closely contested by the two parties than in any election afterward.[16] This was not so much a matter of a nation of uniform feelings, but of a divided nation—divided, as always, in partisan politics—with two robust streams of party-switching simultaneously surging in opposite directions. As it turned out, the 1976 election was very far from being the wave of the future and was more a vestige of the past. It was the last time a Democratic presidential candidate won a majority of the popular vote in the once "Solid South" and the last time a Republican presidential candidate came close to winning what would have been the decisive electoral votes of New York. The familiar partisan patterns prevailing in non-landslide reelection years since World War II would be altered in the 1980s, to Republicans' advantage, and again in the 1990s, to the advantage of the Democrats.

This change was ushered in by a period of policy unsuccess. The eight years starting in 1973 saw economic woes and political instability not experienced before in the postwar years. One president, facing impeachment and removal, resigned his office, and two successive presidents were defeated for reelection. The level of unemployment and inflation combined—stagflation—increased beyond what economists had considered possible; wage and price controls, imposed to provide order, created disorder instead, most visibly in the lines outside gas stations in 1973 and 1979. Americans seemed in retreat abroad, as the last U.S. helicopters left the embassy in South Vietnam, and Soviet military strength seemed to increase while the American military declined. And when Iranian "students" seized U.S. embassy personnel in Tehran—a violation of the first fundamental rule of international law—the Carter administration was unable to do more than to order a rescue attempt that failed and to send Christmas presents in the hopes that they would melt the hearts of the revolutionary Islamist mullahs governing the nation. The genuine original achievements of the Carter administration—deregulation of freight rail, truck, and air transportation; a peace agreement between Israel and Egypt—were overshadowed by crises while Americans watched the 1980 presidential campaign.

Throughout the campaign it was apparent that Jimmy Carter would not win the kind of landslide reelection that postwar presidents had won in 1956 (57 percent), 1964 (61 percent), and 1972 (61 percent). Poll results during the campaign were volatile, and while Carter was ahead at various points, his support was connected to his efforts to free the hostages in Iran, which in the end proved unavailing. But on election night the result came as a shock: Carter won just 41 percent of the vote. He carried only six states plus the District of Columbia: his home state and his vice president's; two jurisdictions with large black populations and high government employment, D.C. and Maryland; and three diverse states with heavily Democratic blue-collar workers, Rhode Island, West Virginia, and Hawaii. He lost some normally Democratic constituencies because of stands on particular issues—always a potential problem for the nominee of a party with a highly diverse coalition—including Jewish voters in New York and south Florida unhappy with the pressure he put on Israel in the Camp David negotiations, midwestern farmers unhappy with his embargo on Soviet wheat exports, westerners miffed with his administration's environmental restrictions. Carter was also hurt by the third-party candidacy of John Anderson, a twenty-year congressman from Illinois and employer of the future Reagan budget director David Stockman. Though a Republican, Anderson was something of a cultural liberal, whose 7 percent of the electorate surely took many more votes from Carter than Reagan. Anderson's performance was yet another example of the fading away of liberal Republicans—even though for most of his years in Congress his voting record wasn't very liberal.

Ronald Reagan, who carried 44 states in this election and would carry 49 four years later, was long considered a right-wing extremist, unelectable, incapable of governing in a complex modern society—despite his considerable success as governor of the nation's largest state for eight years. Reagan had campaigned for governor as a citizen-politician and for president as an outsider, concealing the considerable knowledge of public policy and sure political instincts revealed in the handwritten radio scripts discovered by the historian Kiron Skinner.[17] Underestimated by his Democratic opponent in California, Edmund G. (Pat) Brown, and by his Republican rival Richard Nixon, he seems to have impressed the shrewd Dwight Eisenhower, whom he met during the former president's winters in Palm Springs and with whom he maintained a substantive correspondence, as Gene Kopelson, an amateur historian, has discovered and documented.[18] In the 1960s, Reagan was dismissed as a radical in the Goldwater mold, while Eisenhower was lauded as a realistic liberal rather than one who concealed his conservatism until after his retirement. (Goldwater's poor showing in 1964, it may be noted, was due largely to Lyndon Johnson getting credit for peace and prosperity and to voters' unwillingness to upset things less than a year after the assassination of John Kennedy.)

Reagan's majority in 1980 looked very much like Eisenhower's in 1952. Both Republicans ran about even in the Outer South, ahead in southern cities and behind in the rural Deep South; both carried large states in the Northeast and the industrial Midwest by less than their national average, with their best showings in affluent suburbs; both were strongest in the Great Plains and the Rocky Mountains. Reagan got 55.3 percent of the major-party vote in 1980, almost exactly the same as Eisenhower's 55.4 percent of the major-party vote in 1952. Reagan was renominated without opposition in 1984—the first incumbent president unopposed in primaries and caucuses since Eisenhower in 1956. Both resembled Franklin Roosevelt, whom Reagan always supported, in projecting an image of being friendly and open—and in having no close friends or associates whom they fully trusted.[19] Eisenhower was the first and Reagan the last incumbent president who, having seemed to produce peace and prosperity, was reelected in a landslide by an electorate dominated by those with living memories of the Great Depression and World War II. Reagan, like Eisenhower, did not win quite everywhere. He trailed in blue-collar areas left behind in the decade's buoyant economic growth—in the coal and steel country of western Pennsylvania and northeast Ohio—and in farm country in Iowa. His margins in both affluent and modest-income suburbs enabled him to carry most large metropolitan areas (exceptions: university-heavy Boston and San Francisco, industrial Pittsburgh and Cleveland, government-heavy Washington).

This success was followed by the election of Reagan's vice president, George H. W. Bush, in 1988—the only time since 1945 that one party has won the presidency three times in a row. Both parties in 1988 had sharply contested primaries, and Reagan stayed aloof from supporting Bush or any other Republican. The poll numbers oscillated wildly: during the summer, the Democratic nominee, Michael Dukakis, led Bush by 17 percent; by September, Bush forged to a smaller but steadier lead. Democrats in this period had the disadvantage of supporting unpopular positions: the nominee in 1984, Walter Mondale (Jimmy Carter's vice president), had vowed to repeal the Reagan tax cuts and raise tax rates; in 1988, Dukakis opposed the death penalty and had supported weekend furloughs for prisoners sentenced to life without parole. Violent crime rates and welfare dependency had roughly tripled in the decade between 1965 and 1975 and plateaued or even rose through the late 1980s. Democrats' opposition to more intensive policing and tougher penalties for criminals and tighter limits on welfare benefits were widely unpopular, especially in major metropolitan areas where stories about violent crime were featured on local newscasts night after night. As a consequence, metro areas that had produced Democratic margins since the 1930s started voting Republican in presidential elections.

But not necessarily in congressional elections. Democratic candidates might—in most cases, did—support those unpopular positions, but Democrats nevertheless held majorities in the House of Representatives in every biennial election from 1954 up through 1994 and in the Senate in all but six years (1980–86) of this forty-year period. In the beginning of this period, this dominance of Congress owed much to the Democrats' near-monopoly of southern seats, but starting with the off-year election in recessionary 1958, Democrats held at least 243 seats in the 435-member House, and in recessionary and Watergate-affected 1974 they won a supermajority of 295. In 1954 only a minority of congressional Democrats were liberals—that is, politicians who supported something like Franklin Roosevelt's Second Bill of Rights. After 1958 the number approached a majority, and many of them began urging the party's congressional leaders to impose discipline on the Democratic Caucus, to provide majorities for measures that otherwise fell short. Members like Richard Bolling and James Roosevelt urged Speaker Sam Rayburn to curb the autonomy of committee chairmen chosen by seniority and to penalize Democrats who voted against liberal measures. They were struggling to make the Democrats a uniformly liberal party, as urged by Franklin Roosevelt and political scientists like E. E. Schattschneider and Samuel Beer.

Liberals gained ground slowly in the 1960s, as the Kennedy and Johnson administrations and the AFL-CIO became aggressive leaders on issues that Rayburn and his successor, John McCormack, usually hesitated to promote. Democratic members, meanwhile, began to use the advantages of incumbency and constituency service to win reelection even in years unfavorable to their party,[20] and maintained large Democratic majorities even after the plurality election of Richard Nixon

in 1968 and his landslide reelection in 1972. Younger Democrats especially joined the Democratic Study Group, founded in 1959, guided in
the 1970s by Phillip Burton, a veteran of the left-wing politics of the
San Francisco docks. His great triumph came in the off-year election in
1974, just three months after Richard Nixon was forced to resign and two
months after Gerald Ford pardoned him. The backlash against Watergate
hurt Republicans, especially in the nonmetropolitan Midwest, where
Republicans traditionally were regarded as more honest and trustworthy than Democrats, and so did the macroeconomy, as inflation raged,
unemployment ballooned, and gasoline prices sped upward. Democrats
in the Watergate years—1972 through 1976—fielded dozens of young,
liberal, politically adept candidates, groomed by Burton and his allies,
who were elected in conservative-leaning districts and who used local
issues and constituency services to hold on to Republican-leaning seats
for the better part of two decades.[21]

After the Democrats' off-year triumph, Burton and the "Watergate
babies" implemented significant reforms—notably, secret-ballot election
of committee and major subcommittee chairmen by the Democratic
Caucus instead of automatic selection according to seniority. Three
committee chairmen were ousted (William Poage of Agriculture, Wright
Patman of Banking, F. Edward Hébert of Armed Services), and the lesson was apparent to others: you must assemble a liberal voting record on
the floor and in committee if you want to be chairman. Oldtimers like
Jamie Whitten of Mississippi, first elected weeks before Pearl Harbor
and in line for the chair of the Appropriations Committee, immediately adjusted his voting record from hard-shell conservative to mostly
liberal. The Rules Committee, controlled since the 1930s by a coalition
of conservative Democrats and Republicans, now had two-thirds of its
members appointed by the Democratic leadership. This meant that the
leadership seldom brought to the floor any measures not supported by
a majority of Democrats, and usually the rules limited amendments so
as to favor liberal results. Democratic leaders allowed members with
conservative constituencies to vote their districts on final roll calls, but
made sure they voted with the leadership on rules.

This new order of things did not inevitably produce liberal results,
but it tended to. Democrats' persistent majorities also enabled their
members to raise much more in the way of campaign funds than could

Republican challengers. "Just remember that we hold every committee and every subcommittee chairmanship," the head of their campaign committee reminded lobbyists, "and we know how to count."

CHAPTER 12

How Partisan Polarized Parity
Came into Being

By 1990 it was widely held by political journalists that Republicans had a "lock" on the presidency and Democrats a "lock" on the House of Representatives. Pundits and political scientists identified structural advantages that Republicans had in presidential elections and Democrats in congressional elections—advantages they were confident would persist for years and perhaps decades to come. As it turned out, they didn't: just when political trends and their causes are identified, they often tend to disappear. I remember speaking to a group of House Democrats in 1990 and arguing that these "locks" might get picked in the coming decade, and so the 1990s might see the election of President Bill Bradley—I, or maybe the country, picked the wrong Bill—and Speaker Newt Gingrich. At that point a groan came from the vicinity of John Dingell, who was on the verge of becoming the longest-serving member of Congress and ended up maintaining that status longer than anyone else in history. Since my talk, Democrats have won four of the seven presidential elections starting in 1992 and Republicans have won majorities in the House of Representatives in ten of thirteen congressional elections starting in 1994. The old "locks" are history.

The first lock to be picked was the Republicans' supposed lock on the presidency. The idea was that with Republicans now sweeping the South and always carrying California (as they had, with the single exception of 1964, between 1952 and 1988), they were assured of something like

215 electoral votes, and were far ahead in almost all the Great Plains and Rocky Mountain states' 70 electoral votes. This analysis was not airtight. Some southern states, economically and demographically, were coming to resemble northern states open to voting Democratic, and Republicans carried California only by single digits in the close elections of 1960, 1968, and 1976, and in the not-so-close election of 1988.

Nevertheless, Democrats who were raised to consider themselves the natural majority party were nevertheless enormously frustrated at losing five of the six presidential elections from 1968 to 1988, and by an average of 10 percent of the popular vote. In the three presidential elections of the 1980s, they carried a total of only 17 states out of 150 cumulatively up for grabs. Despite their continued majorities in the House of Representatives and most state legislatures during this period, this protracted failure at the national level eventually prompted rethinking the national party's stands. The shrewdest effort came from Bill Clinton, governor of Arkansas, and the Democratic Leadership Council founded by Al From, a former congressional staffer. They recognized that Democrats' stands on crime and welfare dependency were responsible for losing almost every crime-ridden metropolitan area, and that Democrats' dovish statements on foreign policy were unsustainable politically as the United States won the Cold War and the Soviet Union ceased to exist. In early 1991 the Democrats seemed destined to lose a fourth election in a row. After the American victory in the Gulf War—which Senate Democrats, still in the grip of Vietnam, almost unanimously opposed—George Bush's job approval peaked at 91 percent, and prominent Democrats like Mario Cuomo, the governor of New York, declined to run. Bill Clinton entered the race that fall, while tacitly admitting his frequent philandering.

But the unexpected happened. In February 1992, the Texas celebrity billionaire Ross Perot launched an independent candidacy, bemoaning Bush's NAFTA trade agreement with Mexico and Canada. In the words of a Democratic strategist, Perot "de-partisanized the critique of Bush" in a way that Clinton, struggling through the gauntlet of Democratic primaries, could not. In June, Perot led polls in a three-way race, with Clinton running third. But in July, Perot dropped out of the race on the third day of the Democratic National Convention and Clinton's support rose 25 points. The Republican leads that appeared so steady in four of the five elections of the last 25 years now seemed to vanish. Perot reentered the race in October, and despite his weird conduct he won 9 percent of the popular vote; he carried no states but ran second in Maine and Utah. Bush, who had won 53 percent four years before (more than anyone since then), got only 37 percent this time—a decline in percentage comparable to that of Herbert Hoover during the Great Depression. Clinton won 43 percent and a solid 370 electoral votes, including 253 from 22 states Bush had carried in 1988. But the electorate was very much split: Clinton got more than 50 percent only in his own state of Arkansas and the District of Columbia; Bush and Perot ran under 50 percent everywhere.

In many ways the Perot candidacy resembled the Trump candidacy 24 years later. Both were widely known as successful entrepreneurs; both decried the free-trade policies of both major parties and questioned the worth of foreign alliances and military interventions. Both campaigned bombastically and disregarded traditional political customs. Both zoomed to leads in the polls, Perot against both major party nominees within four months of announcing, Trump against sixteen Republican rivals within two months of announcing. But Perot stumbled, and his defeat may have shown Trump the unwisdom of running an independent candidacy, however tenuous his ties to either major party, and certainly demonstrated the unwisdom of abandoning his supporters by dropping out of the race and then hopping back in.

The patterns of partisan support in the 1992 election were significantly different from those that had prevailed in most of the country since 1952 and in the South except for those years with a southern Democratic or third-party candidate. Clinton's overall percentage mostly trailed that of Michael Dukakis in the two-way contest four years earlier, but the articulate Clinton ran significantly better in both upscale and blue-collar suburbs in the largest metropolitan areas and urban conglomerations—New York, Chicago, Los Angeles and San Francisco, South Florida. Clinton's promise to end "welfare as we know it" and his firm disapproval of violent crime fared much better in those high-crime, high-welfare areas than Dukakis's tendency to see welfare recipients and criminals as victims of racism or inequality. At the same time, Clinton's support of abortion "rights" appealed to cultural liberals who feared that Reagan and Bush nominees would overturn the Supreme Court's *Roe v. Wade* decision (though they declined to do so in the *Casey* decision that June). Clinton's articulateness appealed to the college-educated, while his southern accent and that of his equally young vice presidential choice, Al Gore, enabled Democrats to carry six of the fourteen southern states. This new pattern of support for Democrats would grow stronger when Clinton was reelected in 1996, and in some cases even more so for other Democrats in the twenty-first century.

Within only a few months of when Democrats led by Bill Clinton ended the Republican lock on the presidency, Republicans led by Newt Gingrich ended the Democratic lock on the House of Representatives. Clinton and Gingrich were both Baby Boomers, as defined by William Strauss and Neil Howe in *Generations: The History of America's Future.*[22] Both first ran for Congress unsuccessfully in 1974, and both achieved national notice in 1978 as Clinton was elected governor of Arkansas and Gingrich as the only Republican congressman from Georgia. Both were innovative thinkers and original strategists, politicians of flexibility sometimes indistinguishable from opportunism, but also capable of learning from mistakes. By the middle 1980s, Clinton's skills and connections made him well known to political insiders, while Gingrich's gadfly activities in the House, amplified by C-SPAN, made him well known among congressional conservatives and correspondents.

By 1984, as Reagan was sweeping to reelection, Gingrich began predicting that Republicans would capture a majority in the House; he was wrong through several electoral cycles, but identified the reasons they eventually did. The Watergate-era Democrats, whose abilities to hold conservative districts may have saved Democrats from losing their majorities several times, would either retire, or run for other offices, or die. Southern Democrats would either change parties (as Phil Gramm and Kent Hance did after losing committee posts for supporting the Reagan tax and spending bills), or retire, or die, or (occasionally) be defeated, and would be replaced in almost every case by Republicans more in line with their districts on national issues. Third, when Democrats did have the presidency as well as Congress and could attempt to pass their liberal policies into law, as they were not able to do explicitly when Reagan and Bush were president, they would be unpopular enough to create Republican majorities.

Some of these things began happening in the 1980s: retirements and deaths, a few defeats, an ebbing of Democratic support in the South. In 1989, when Dick Cheney resigned from the House to become secretary of defense, Gingrich was elected to succeed him as minority whip—by just two votes. But his election undercut the minority leader, Robert Michel, and legitimized Gingrich's role as the House Republicans' chief electoral and policy strategist. In 1990, even as Republicans lost a little ground nationally, they won a higher percentage of the House popular vote in the South than in the North, for the first time since Reconstruction; they have continued to be stronger in the South in every election since. Finally, in 1994 the correlation of forces for Gingrich's revolution fell into place. Hillary Clinton's failed health-care proposals seemed to many voters a revival of big-government policies they thought they had left behind, while Clinton's tax increases passed by Democratic votes antagonized high-income suburban voters. Gingrich recruited candidates all across the country and got them in September to endorse a "Contract with America," pledging mainly procedural reforms. On Election Day, Republicans won a majority in the Senate and gained 54 seats in the House, for their first majority (230-205) since 1952.

As Speaker-designate, Gingrich pushed through the Republican Conference a series of party reforms eerily similar to those pushed through the Democratic Caucus by Phil Burton twenty years before. Chairmen of committees and Appropriations subcommittees would be elected by a steering committee, on which the Speaker, the majority leader, and the whip would have multiple votes and choose other members. Term limits of six years would be imposed on chairmanships, assuring constant rotation in office and incentives for would-be chairmen to raise money for colleagues' campaigns. Just as Burton's reforms had created the reliably liberal party that Franklin Roosevelt called for, Gingrich's reforms created the reliably conservative party that Roosevelt foresaw as its inevitable opposition.

By 1996 the patterns that would prevail for at least two decades were largely set. Clinton was reelected with 49 percent of the vote, and Republicans won the popular vote for the House of Representatives by a 49 to 48 percent margin. In three of the next five presidential elections, Democrats received between 48 and 51 percent of the votes and Republicans between 46 and 51 percent. In ten of the thirteen House elections from 1994 to 2016, Republicans received between 48 and 52 percent of the popular vote, and Democrats between 44 and 49 percent. There was a decided move away from Republicans and toward Democrats that produced a Democratic House majority in 2006 and a 53 to 46 percent victory for Barack Obama in 2008, plus what amounted to Democratic supermajorities in Congress in 2009–10. But in 2010 and 2012, the 1994–2004 patterns were back in place. This was a period of persistent partisan polarization and parity of a length unprecedented in American history, following a quarter century of ticket splitting and vast partisan swings.

In this period, cultural issues—on many of which there had never been partisan dispute, most notably abortion—were determinants of partisan allegiance, and the demographic factor most highly correlated with voting behavior was religion, or degree of religiosity, with the most religious in each sectarian group leaning Republican, and the least religious leaning Democratic. The Republican core group was no longer northern white Protestants—many of the more affluent among them now voting heavily Democratic—but could be described as white married people, with a heavier concentration in the South than in the North, and more in areas well outside the million-plus metropolises than in their affluent suburbs. The Democratic Party depended increasingly on nonwhites, particularly blacks but also Hispanics and Asians; and on white college graduates, especially single women. In the 1940s and 1950s, affluent Americans outside the South (and increasingly in the South as well) voted overwhelmingly for Republicans, and in presidential and many other elections they would continue to do so by lesser margins until the 1990s. But as cultural issues came to overshadow economics for these and other voters, affluent and college-educated Americans trended Democratic, to a point that would have astonished the New Dealers: The 2008 exit poll showed Barack Obama carrying voters in the highest ($200,000+) income bracket over John McCain, and the 2016 election returns showed Hillary Clinton carrying many affluent neighborhoods by more than two-to-one margins over Donald Trump.

Because many of these Democratic-trending groups were becoming a rising percentage of the national electorate, predictions were made of an "emerging Democratic majority": in the 2002 book of that name by Ruy Teixeira and John Judis, in the journalism of Ronald Brownstein in the *National Journal* and the *Atlantic*, in the pollster Stanley Greenberg's book *Ascendant America*. The demographic clustering of these heavily

Democratic groups in central cities, sympathetic suburbs, and university towns gave Democrats an advantage in the Electoral College, but gave Republicans an advantage in congressional and legislative elections in equal-population districts.

The best guide to political predictions often seemed to be the past election: in the still-fluid politics of the early 1990s, five states switched 57 electoral votes between the 1992 and 1996 presidential elections; between 2000 and 2004, only three states with 16 electoral votes did so; between 2008 and 2012, the switchers were two states with 26. And the focus of the Electoral College shifted as well. In the first half of the twentieth century, New York and some large states that resembled it cast the key electoral votes in closely contested elections. From the 1960s through the 1980s it was the South—in particular, white southern conservatives, who swung the key electoral votes in such races. By the end of the 1990s and into the twenty-first century, the key electoral votes were cast in the industrial Midwest and the kindred state of Pennsylvania, and most visibly in Florida, where many voters had grown up in the aforementioned states, or in New York or the South when they were successively the fulcrum of American politics.

Donald Trump's victory in the 2016 presidential contest, though almost entirely unpredicted, did not represent a major change from the polarized partisan patterns. Trump ran significantly better than previous Republicans among white non college-graduates and significantly worse among white college graduates. The differences were not overwhelming, however, and in terms of popular votes those differences tended basically to cancel each other out. He lost the popular vote by 2 percent, the average for Republican nominees in the previous four presidential races. But the electoral-vote count was different. Trump's weak showing among white college graduates resulted in worse Republican showings in states including California, Arizona, Colorado, Texas, and Georgia—worse percentages, but no loss of electoral votes as compared with 2008 or 2012. In effect there was a movement toward Democrats among the college-educated in metro Atlanta, Dallas, Houston, and Phoenix, similar to what occurred starting in the mid-1990s in most non-southern metro areas.

But Trump's relatively strong showings among white non-college-graduate voters in Florida, Pennsylvania, Ohio, Michigan, Wisconsin, Iowa, and the 2nd congressional district of Maine—voters whom Democratic strategists, in their concentration on "ascendant" nonwhites and young singles, took for granted—resulted in a net gain of 100 electoral votes over 2008 and 2010 for Republicans. Hillary Clinton ran far behind Barack Obama's showings in the nonmetropolitan parts of these states. That may owe something to the contempt she showed for "deplorables." But the Obama benchmark may have been unusually high, particularly in large parts of the Midwest where there were traditions in both parties of support for black rights and aspirations— among Republicans, dating from the foundations of their party in the 1850s; among Democrats, dating from the rise of the industrial unions in the 1930s. In any case, a small shift in votes by members of demographic groups—similar in magnitude to the shifts among such groups between the postwar close elections of 1960, 1968, and 1976—had large consequences in personnel and policy. And if Donald Trump seemed to diverge from past Republican nominees and presidents on issues like trade and foreign policy, such divergences have not been unknown in the history of either of America's major parties.

Whatever the divergences of Donald Trump from other Republican nominees—and they do not seem historically unprecedented—they did not prevent him from winning near-unanimous support from Republican voters. The force of partisanship—the residual strength of the two ancient American parties—seemed undiminished and perhaps stronger than ever.

Trump's election may have exacerbated the bitterness of political rhetoric, but it did not mark the beginning of the fulfillment of Franklin Roosevelt's dream of two ideologically distinct political parties. The prayers of the postwar political scientists have been fully answered—to the regret of the large majority of today's political scientists and commentators and, perhaps, practitioners. Whether Trump will be reelected is unclear as this is written; how and when post-Trump Democrats will govern remains utterly unknown.

It bears remembering, amid the harsh partisan clangor, that for most of the forty years from 1952 to 1992, when Republicans dominated presidential elections, Democrats held majorities in Congress, and that for most of the years since 1992, when Democrats have dominated presidential elections, albeit by smaller margins, Republicans have held majorities in Congress. If Americans from the Civil War up through World War II were inclined to entrust the executive and legislatives branches to one party, since World War II they have usually been inclined to entrust one branch to one party and the other to the other. But through it all, the parties have been a force for stability, for channeling public opinion and enthusiasm and discontent into relatively familiar and navigable channels. Rather than regret our partisanship and disparage our two ancient political parties, we should seek to build on their strengths and cherish their formidable heritages.

III

The Parties in Regions

CHAPTER 13

The South

In August 2017, I watched, through welder's glasses, the total eclipse of the sun on the front lawn of Fort Hill, John C. Calhoun's mansion in Clemson, South Carolina. I had driven from Washington to Fort Hill—which is on the campus of Clemson University, founded by Calhoun's son-in-law Thomas Clemson—through some 500 miles of territory, across the invisible boundary between North and South, and over and around the mountain chains that divide the Tidewater South from the Appalachian South. My journey got me thinking about the differences between the North and the South, especially the differences in their politics, how southern politics has developed over the years—and where it stands now.

The first thing to realize is that the South has been distinctive from the very beginning. The canonical book on the subject, V. O. Key's *Southern Politics*, on its first page declares that "the South remains the region with the most distinctive character and tradition." Key emphasizes that "the politics of the South is incredibly complex. Its variety, its nuances, its subtleties range across the political spectrum." A valid point, illustrated by the 675 pages that follow. "Further," he says, "the South is changing rapidly," as indeed it was when he was writing in the 1940s.[23]

But the distinctiveness of southern politics, and of the South, goes much further back. The historian Henry Adams, writing in the 1890s about America in 1800, describes the citizens of the young American

Republic as "one people," English-speaking, almost all Protestant, largely descended from settlers from the British Isles. Yet one of his first chapters is entitled "Intellect of the Southern States," which he describes as far different from the intellect of the New England states and the Middle states.[24]

Adams's point was made more fully a century later by David Hackett Fischer in his book *Albion's Seed*, which describes how the different British North American colonies were settled by peoples from distinct parts of the British Isles, who brought their religion and their culture and their sexual mores—their folkways—with them. The Chesapeake colonies, Fischer writes, were settled by Cavaliers from the West Country of England, by gentlemen used to hierarchical deference and by small farmers, indentured servants and, later, slaves imported from Africa, who readily granted it. The Virginian elite, he wrote, cherished liberty as "a hegemonic condition of dominion over others and—equally important—dominion over oneself."[25] Charleston and the Carolina Low Country is a variant of this, with a constitution crafted by the liberty-loving philosopher John Locke and an economy based on the model of slaveholding Barbados. A century or more later came the fighting men and women of the violent borderlands of North Britain, especially Lowland Scotland and Northern Ireland. Arriving in Philadelphia, they traveled down the Shenandoah Valley in the Great Wagon Road—much the same route I took to Fort Hill—to the Appalachian mountains and beyond. Among their number were talented and bold men who led in battle and land development, like the forebears of Andrew Jackson and John C. Calhoun, born in the Up Country of South Carolina in 1767 and 1782. Such men had "a strong attachment to their liberties," Fischer writes, quoting an eighteenth-century traveler who said, "They shun everything which appears to demand of them law and order, and anything that preaches constraint, and yet they are not transgressors.... Natural freedom ... is what pleases them."[26]

Using the times of the early Republic, the times that Adams and Fischer are describing, as a starting point, I want to describe southern politics in what I believe are five distinct periods, showing how it developed and how it was distinctive from that of the rest of the nation in each. I start with the early period of the Republic, in which the United States chose presidents from Virginia for 32 of 36 years, up until the middle 1820s. The next period I call the antebellum South, when the tremendous economic success of the slave-manned cotton industry that dominated southern culture had center stage in the political drama—a period that ends of course with what some south of Washington insist on calling the War Between the States. The third period is the 75 years—three-quarters of a century—between the Civil War and World War II, when the South is literally a land apart, and Americans southern and northern live as visibly separated from each other as if divided by a wall. The fourth period is one in which a seemingly unchanging South is transformed—by war, by the northward migration of one-third of American blacks, by the civil rights movement and the reaction thereto. This period lasts only 25 years, one generation, but has profound effects. And finally, my fifth period covers the last 50 years, from the middle 1960s, and seems to be stretching forward into the future. It is a period in which the South has been growing as a percentage of the nation's population and economy, and in which its distinctiveness is actually less vivid and more muted than ever before—but still readily perceptible, and perceived, and pronounced particularly in our politics.

I.

When we think about the differences between South and North, our first focus is inevitably on the Civil War and on the issue that Lincoln said in his second inaugural address was the "peculiar and powerful interest" that was "somehow the cause of the war": slavery. But if you put yourself back in the time of the Declaration of Independence in 1776, the picture looks different. Slavery was legal in every one of the thirteen colonies. It was abolished in 1777 in Vermont, at that time an independent nation, and in 1780 in Quaker-founded Pennsylvania. Partial or total abolition followed in the New England states in 1783 and 1784, in New York in 1799 and New Jersey in 1804, and many hoped that precedent would move farther south. There was no visible dissent when Congress in 1807 prohibited the international slave trade effective January 1, 1808, the earliest date allowed in the Constitution. It seemed, as many of the Founders had hoped, that slavery might gradually wither away just about everywhere but the Low Country of South Carolina.

What dashed those hopes was cotton. No other fiber, natural or synthetic, has proved so useful or popular in clothing and dry goods, and in the 1780s entrepreneurs and inventors in England were developing the spinning jenny and water frame and building giant textile mills. They needed a supply of raw cotton, and found one after Eli Whitney, on a sojourn in Savannah in 1793, invented the cotton gin, which was fifty times more efficient at removing cotton seeds than hand labor. The American South—especially the Black Belt of rich soil across Georgia, Alabama, and Mississippi—was ideal land for growing cotton. Prices of cotton land tripled, and American cotton production increased exponentially. "The countryside was turned upside down," writes the historian Sven Beckert, "from a thinly inhabited region of native people and farmers who focused on subsistence crops and tobacco to one in thrall to cotton."[27] The most efficient way to grow cotton was with slave labor, and so Atlantic seaboard slaves were sold and marched off in coffles in a horrific "second middle passage" to the new cotton lands to the west. By 1830 the United States produced half the world's cotton and supplied 70 percent of Britain's cotton imports. Slavery, far from withering on the vine, became the cornerstone of the southern economy, and the nation's slave population increased from less than one million in 1800 to almost four million in 1860.

II.

The economic dependence on slavery gave southern politics a distinctive and increasingly regional cast. As the electorates of the northern states swelled with educated freehold farmers and city-dwelling artisans, southern electorates remained small and dominated by slaveholders. Four of the first five presidents were Virginians and slaveholders, strongly nationalist in outlook, and so were the politicians who jostled to succeed them in the one-party, multicandidate election of 1824. But by the late 1820s, as cotton plantations and slavery spread across the Appalachians and the Mississippi Valley, southern politics became increasingly regional.

A prime example is John C. Calhoun of Up Country South Carolina, elected to Congress in 1810 as a young war hawk eager for what would be the War of 1812. As secretary of war for eight years, Calhoun promoted national expansion and an effective military, appointing the reformer Sylvanus Thayer as commander of West Point. In 1824, at age 42, he passed up a four-candidate presidential race and ran with no serious opposition for vice president.

In that national post, Calhoun became a southern regionalist. He joined Low Country plantation owners in rejecting proposals that would deprive that minority of control of the legislature. He opposed increases in what opponents called the Tariff of Abominations and secretly drafted memoranda arguing that states could nullify federal laws. He intrigued against both presidents with whom he served—John Quincy Adams on the tariff, and Andrew Jackson on nullification. South Carolina backed down on nullification when Jackson sent troops to its borders, though it got lowered tariffs in return.

Calhoun resigned as vice president and the legislature elected him to the Senate, as it would whenever he wanted for the rest of his life. A man of great learning and argumentative skill, he began to proclaim that slavery was a positive good, that southern plantation slaves were better treated than northern mill hands, and that the South had a right to secede if it lacked a veto—what he called a concurrent majority—over laws affecting its basic institutions. Which is what South Carolina did in December 1860, followed by ten other states in early 1861, when the Republican Party, which did not even distribute ballots in the South, had captured the presidency. And, as Lincoln said in his second inaugural address, the war came.

III.

Let me pass over the Civil War and Reconstruction, the decade-long effort by Republicans to promote equal rights for blacks in the South, as episodes that are broadly familiar. I want to make one overriding point about the politics of the South after the war: in the 75 years from 1865 to 1940, with only the briefest and most minor exceptions, the South and the North were like two unfriendly nations living apart, as if there were a wall along the Potomac and Ohio rivers. Before the war there had been significant migration between South and North: Abraham Lincoln, born in Kentucky, raised in Indiana, thriving in Illinois, was a typical example; so were the northern-born John Slidell and Robert Walker, who made successful political careers in Louisiana and Mississippi. After the war there was scarcely any interregional movement. While some thirty million Europeans ventured across the Atlantic Ocean to settle in the North, only one million whites and one million blacks from the South did so—even though northern wage levels were twice as high as southern wages. The rapid industrialization and economic growth of the North scarcely touched the South, where manufacturing was limited to the cigarette factories and textile mills of North Carolina and the steel plant beneath the iron ore mountain that flanks Birmingham, Alabama.

Nor did antebellum southern party politics carry over into the postbellum years. Antebellum southern politics evolved from battles between local chieftains—Tennessee's Andrew Jackson versus Kentucky's Henry Clay—to contests between the same two parties that competed in the North, in which the Whigs tended to carry counties with big plantations while Democrats won those with smaller farmers. But after the war, southerners voted as they had voted on secession and as they had fought during the war. Blacks voted overwhelmingly Republican when and where they were allowed to vote—which by the 1890s meant only in a few cities like Louisville and Richmond. Most whites voted Democratic, the party that opposed Abraham Lincoln, while regions that had opposed secession—east Tennessee, much of West Virginia, isolated pockets like the "free state" of Winston County, Alabama—remained faithfully Republican. The region came to be known as the Solid South, solidly Democratic. That's an oversimplified picture: the North was more Republican than the South, but not by wide margins, while the Upper South—Virginia, West Virginia, North Carolina, Kentucky, Tennessee, Arkansas—was not so very much different, voting between 40 and 50 percent Republican through most of the period. In contrast, the Lower South, with very low turnout because ballot restrictions barred blacks and deterred poor whites, typically voted 75 to 85 percent Democratic.

Overall the South became detached from presidential politics, with southern states achieving target status only occasionally (for example, the McKinley campaign targeted Kentucky and Tennessee in 1896). Southerners were considered unsuitable as presidential candidates: Woodrow Wilson may have grown up in Virginia, Georgia, and South Carolina, but he ran as a son of New Jersey, and the only southern vice presidential nominee from 1865 to 1924 was the 81-year-old West Virginia millionaire Henry Gassaway Davis in 1904. In 1928 and the 1930s, Democrats nominated southerners, Joseph Robinson of Arkansas and John Nance Garner of Texas, as ticket balancers to their New York presidential nominees, Al Smith and Franklin Roosevelt. State politics remained out of touch with national elections, with turnout often higher in Democratic primaries than in general elections. The popularity among southern whites of Franklin Roosevelt's New Deal and wartime leadership pushed Democratic percentages notably higher than in the 1865–1930 period, so that political journalists and even political scientists as shrewd as V. O. Key portrayed the South as overwhelmingly Democratic, and concentrated on describing the particularities of the one-party politics that developed in the different southern states.

Northern voters in the 1870s forced the abandonment of Reconstruction and turned their eyes away from the segregation institutionalized by politicians and enforced by threats of violence in the South. When Republican presidents even suggested enforcing equal rights for blacks—Theodore Roosevelt inviting Booker T. Washington to lunch in 1902, Warren Harding calling for equal rights in Birmingham, Alabama, in 1921—they were bitterly denounced throughout the South, and they backed off. When the sociologist John Dollard published *Caste and Class in a Southern Town* in 1937, based on six months of research in Indianola, Mississippi, it was hailed as a revelation by northern academics. Yet the practices and customs it documented were known to any six-year-old, black or white, in the South.

IV.

Once again, in the 1940s, as in the 1860s, the war came, with profound effects on the South. Even before Pearl Harbor, Congress in August 1940 authorized the military draft, which would eventually put in uniform 16 million Americans in a nation of 131 million. Northern factories were converted to military production, and managers desperate for workers went recruiting south of that invisible wall that had separated South from North for the preceding 75 years—recruiting blacks as well as whites. Franklin Roosevelt, on the advice of his military leaders, refused to integrate the segregated military, but under pressure from A. Philip Randolph he issued a fair-employment executive order banning racial discrimination in defense industries. The war literally mixed Americans together and, in the words of the military historian Thomas Bruscino, "taught them to get along."[28]

In the process, it got the South looking at the North and the North looking at the South. Those looking northward mostly liked what they saw. In the 25 years from 1940 to 1965, about one-third of American blacks moved from the (mostly rural) South to the urban North, and perhaps as many southern whites moved north and west as well. At the same time, the war brought forward a strong argument for equal treatment of blacks: if they could die for their country, they ought to be treated equally by their country. This prompted President Harry Truman to set up a civil rights commission and to order desegregation of the military, carried forward by Dwight Eisenhower. The 1948 Democratic National Convention adopted a civil rights plank, which led to the States' Rights Democratic candidacy of Strom Thurmond, who won 39 electoral votes, all but one of them from the four Deep South states with the highest percentages of blacks: South Carolina, Alabama, Mississippi, and Louisiana.

The large majorities of white southerners opposed to changes in state segregation laws and practices was not the only factor pushing the South away from its record levels of support for Democrats in the presidential elections of 1932 to 1944. Early New Deal programs were popular there, and farm subsidy programs continued to be so, while white southerners opposed policies promoting national labor unions and welfare spending. On foreign policy issues, the South was the strongest region for military preparedness before World War II and for an internationalist policy afterward; that made little difference when both parties supported the bipartisan Cold War policy in the twenty years from 1947 to 1967, but it gave Republicans a distinct advantage in the decades afterward. Southern Democrats in Congress reflected these views, forming part of a conservative coalition that mostly prevailed in congressional majorities from 1938 to 1958 and continuing to buck liberal northern Democrats afterward.

The 1952 election saw the first significant expansion of the national electorate since 1940, from 49 million to 62 million, and in the South from 7.5 million to 11.4 million. The Republican nominee, Dwight Eisenhower, won 49 percent of the vote in the South in 1952 and 50 percent in 1956—a level maintained by the Republican nominee in 1960, Richard Nixon. To their traditional mountain areas, Republicans added the South's suddenly growing and relatively prosperous cities, from

Houston and Dallas, to Miami and Tampa, to Richmond and Louisville and Charlotte, and to Charleston, Columbia, and Greenville in South Carolina. This was a vote of the upward middle class, moderate on race. The same pattern recurred in 1956 and 1960, and again in the three-way race including Alabama's George Wallace as the American Independent Party candidate in 1968.

Quite different was the behavior of the rural and small-town Lower South, where whites most strongly supported segregation. These counties voted for Strom Thurmond, States' Rights Democrat, in 1948; for Barry Goldwater, the Republican, after his vote against the Civil Rights Act in 1964; for George Wallace in 1968. By that time, legally enforced segregation was becoming a lost cause; effective desegregation of schools was on the brink of being accomplished by the Nixon administration.

V.

Another difference between the parties emerged in the fifth period: hawks versus doves. On this issue, white southerners overwhelmingly favored the hawkish Republican position, as reflected in 1972, when Nixon won 70 percent of the southern vote over the dovish George McGovern, who carried only 35 of the region's 1,394 counties (none of them casting as many as 20,000 votes).

Thanks to the hugely effective Voting Rights Act of 1965, black voters were now fully a part of the southern electorate, and voting overwhelmingly Democratic. This resulted in the election of dozens and ultimately hundreds of black local officials and state legislators and, as early as 1972, in the election of black congressmen in Houston and in a white-majority district of Atlanta. And white southerners were not entirely detached from the Democratic Party; we can see their presidential voting choices, oscillating from one party and candidate to another, as seeking the candidate most in line with their views. In 1976 they switched toward Jimmy Carter, the Democratic governor of Georgia who hung a portrait of Martin Luther King, Jr. in the state capitol, a graduate of the Naval Academy who proclaimed himself a born-again Christian in the midst of a decade when cultural issues like abortion emerged into partisan politics. Carter carried the North by 0.4 percent but carried the South with 54 to 42 percent over the Yankee Gerald Ford. It was the last time a Republican presidential nominee would run stronger in the North than in the South. In presidential elections over the four decades that have followed, the South has been the most Republican region in the country.

The South's changing partisan preference in presidential voting was not reflected for years in elections for congressional and state offices. In these contests most southern voters clung to the Democratic Party, in large part because so many southern politicians did so. Well into the 1980s, and in some states until 2010, Democrats had large majorities in most southern legislatures and congressional delegations and in local offices, so if you wanted a political career, it made sense to be a Democrat. You should also not be weighted down with the liberal stands of most Democrats in Congress or the party's presidential nominees. There were alternative Democratic templates of national renown, represented by George Wallace, who ran as an Independent in 1968 but in Democratic presidential primaries in 1964, 1972, and 1976; and by Jimmy Carter, the party's presidential nominee in 1976 and 1980. Democrats remained a majority in the U.S. House of Representatives from 1954 to 1994 and in the U.S. Senate for 34 of those 40 years, and southern Democrats tended to amass great seniority and important committee chairmanships, so they could argue that they were able to serve their constituencies' interests more effectively than a junior Republican stuck in the ranks of the minority. Even as liberals increased their power by establishing caucus election of committee chairmen in 1974, House Democratic leaders took care to allow southern Democrats to cast moderate votes on visible issues, so long as they voted with the leadership on more obscure procedural votes, which often determined legislative outcomes.

So even though southern voters from the 1960s to the 1980s were more conservative than the national average on most economic, military, foreign, and cultural issues, Democrats continued to win the lion's share of popular votes in House elections—62 to 72 percent in the 1960s, 58 to 63 percent in the 1970s, and 55 to 60 percent in the 1980s, a decade in which Democrats won just 44, 37, and 41 percent of southern votes in presidential elections. Change was slow, but clearly in the Republican direction. In 1992, when George H. W. Bush lost the presidency to Bill Clinton, Republicans actually won a higher percentage of the House popular vote in the South than in the North—certainly the first time this had happened since Reconstruction, maybe the first time ever—and held the Democratic vote down to 52 percent.

Then in 1994 came the Republican breakthrough. Republicans won 55 percent of the House popular vote in the South, versus just 51 percent in the North. Since then, Republicans have carried the southern popular vote for the House with between 50 and 60 percent, as white non-college-graduates moved away from ancestral Democratic loyalty and stayed removed. Meanwhile, Republicans have never again equaled the 51 percent of the northern popular vote they won in 1994, as white college-educated voters there, unlike the South, moved toward the Democrats. The same patterns continued for twenty years, in both the South and nationally, with a move away from the Republicans and toward the Democrats in 2006 and 2008, followed by a move back to what looked like the norm.

The 2016 election was different. Not in the South: the vote there changed very little, from a Republican presidential popular-vote margin of 10.1 percent in 2012, to 10.6 percent in 2016. But nationally, a significant number of white college graduates switched away from the Republican ticket while a somewhat larger number of non-college whites shifted away from the Democratic ticket—the same movement observed in congressional and presidential elections in the 1990s—and visible in affluent high-education southern suburbs in 2016. Nationally, this movement had important implications in electoral votes and regional balance. It netted Donald Trump 100 more electoral votes than Mitt Romney had won in 2012. But only 29 of those (Florida's) were in the South, while 70 were in the Midwest and the Rust Belt, with one additional vote coming from Maine.

Southern college-educated voters moved toward Democrats, a movement especially visible in the metro areas of Atlanta, Dallas, and Houston. Non-college whites in the Midwest moved toward Republicans. The result is that the Midwest (at 49–45 Trump) ended up voting much more like the South (53–42 Trump) than like the coasts, the combined Northeast and West (54–39 Clinton). This is the first time we have seen this pattern: the Midwest had voted about the same distance from the coasts as from the South in presidential elections between 1992 and 2012, and virtually identically with the coasts and quite differently from the South up through 1988.

Have the South and the Midwest converged to become a single political region with 57 percent of the nation's popular votes and 298 of its 538 electoral votes (55 percent)? At least temporarily, but possibly just for this one election. On balance, voters in these two formerly politically distinct regions have come to share positions on economic and cultural issues that are sharply different from those that predominate on the coasts. The industrial unions which tilted the Midwest toward Democrats seem to be a spent force, while that region's antislavery and antisegregation tilt is no longer relevant now that no one seeks a return to those old systems in the South. There does remain at least one realm in which the regions' historical heritages could produce political differences. The South has always been supportive of military action. Historically, there have been sharp differences on foreign and military issues between the South, the most hawkish region in the country, and the Midwest, the most dovish.

So the South retains its distinctive character and tradition, and a cultural style of cheerful politeness, more elaborate than that of the Midwest and a sharp contrast with the brusqueness of the coasts. And the particular blend of its people's values and mores still sets it apart. But the political gulf between regions has sharply narrowed, and if future political alignments resemble those of the last presidential election, it may come to be seen as a part—the larger part—of a vast American interior, a majority of the nation, in perennial partisan opposition to the coasts.

CHAPTER 14

The Surprising New Political Battleground: The Midwest‡

Much to the surprise of psephologists—the fancy word for election watchers—the key votes in the 2016 presidential election, putting Donald Trump in the White House, were cast in the Midwest. Not by Hispanics in the Sun Belt or young techies in newly fashionable gentrified neighborhoods in Silicon Valley, Brooklyn, or Austin, but by white non-college-graduates in the counties outside million-plus metropolitan areas in the Midwest. Of the 100 electoral votes that switched from Democratic in 2012 to Republican in 2016, 50 were in the Midwest—Ohio, Michigan, Wisconsin, and Iowa—and 20 were in Pennsylvania, specifically west of metro Philadelphia, which demographically and attitudinally more closely resembles the Midwest than the rest of the Northeast.

An additional 29 of those electoral votes were in Florida, where the key Obama-to-Trump movement came in small counties along the Gulf Coast and north of Orlando heavily inhabited by former midwesterners. One more Democratic-to-Republican electoral vote was that of the 2nd congressional district of Maine, a north-woods area resembling the Upper Peninsula of Michigan or the north woods of Wisconsin and Minnesota. To paraphrase the British tabloid the *Sun*, which headlined

---

‡ This section is based on a lecture that is scheduled to be published, in different form, as part of a book from the University Press of Kansas.

the Conservative Party's surprise 1992 win with "It's the Sun Wot Won It," in 2016 it was the Midwest wot won it.

The standard analysis of this outcome is that significant numbers of white non-college-graduates nationally shifted from Obama to Trump and that those voters were concentrated in the Midwest. That is right, as far as it goes. But history also has its claims—and it can affect voters' attitudes, often almost invisibly, for many years and decades after the fact. So, I want to look at the Midwest's history to explain this unexpected turn of events. And not just to understand why white non-college midwesterners switched from Obama to Trump in 2016, but also to understand why such an unusually high percentage of them, compared with the national average, voted for Obama in 2008 and 2012, and why midwesterners have voted as they have, close to but not identical to the national average, throughout history.

Three pivotal dates in midwestern history—extreme events, as I call them, for what is in retrospect their unusual nature—have shaped midwestern culture and attitudes. They are 1787, 1854, and 1937. Each is far distant to us—232, 165, and 82 years ago. Only a few 2016 midwestern voters were alive for the most recent of these, and almost none grew up with parents who were alive during the second. I add that "almost" caveat because I am aware that the house of President John Tyler, born in 1790, is currently owned by one of his two living grandsons. Tyler was a Virginia planter and slaveholder, not at all a midwesterner, but he was the vice presidential nominee on the Tippecanoe and Tyler Too Whig ticket that carried the Midwest in 1840. History is closer to us than we usually think.

The first date I mentioned, 1787, is usually remembered as the year in which the Constitutional Convention met. But the extreme event I am referring to is another one: the Confederation Congress passed the Northwest Ordinance on July 13, 1787, while the convention was in session down the street in Philadelphia. Modified under criticism by George Washington and by suggestions from James Monroe, the Northwest Ordinance updated Thomas Jefferson's original plan for the territory west of Pennsylvania and north of the Ohio River. It set in motion the relinquishment of eastern states' claims to this territory, sanctioned the eventual admission to the Union of at least three new states there, and—crucially—banned slavery in this new Northwest Territory.

The ban on slavery was an extraordinary measure, virtually unprecedented in the European-American world at that time, and it was adopted at a time when only five of the thirteen original states (Connecticut, Massachusetts, New Hampshire, Pennsylvania, and Rhode Island) had provided for even the gradual abolition of slavery. It has been suggested that tobacco planters in slave states pushed the ban to prevent competition; tobacco can be produced in climates as cold as those of Connecticut and Ontario. Even if its adoption owed something to this cynical calculation, it stands out as an extraordinary and consequential application of the principle declared by the Continental Congress a baker's dozen years earlier: that all men are created equal.

The ban on slavery crucially shaped the culture and economy of the states that to this day contain a majority of midwesterners. The Northwest Ordinance also encouraged land ownership by selling land cheaply to settlers. It encouraged education by setting aside one of sixteen sections of the typical township for schools, and so schools and colleges sprang up, making the Midwest the most educated part of the country. And although much of the Northwest Territory was settled by Virginians and Kentuckians moving down or north over the Ohio River, the Northwest Ordinance discouraged the in-migration of slaveholders and those strongly sympathetic to the peculiar institution. Which is not to say that some of those moving from slave territory into southern Ohio, Indiana, and Illinois did not want their states to join with the one midwestern state outside the Northwest Territory that allowed slavery—Missouri.

This is also not to say that there were not proslavery settlers. In 1824 they made a concerted push to legalize slavery in Illinois, which was defeated by the efforts of Governor Edward Coles, a former White House staffer to James Madison, who had moved his own slaves there from Virginia and bought each family 160 acres of farmland. If Coles had not succeeded, Illinois and midwestern politics might have taken a different turn, the Lincoln-Douglas debates might never have taken place, and Lincoln might have died in obscurity as a successful Springfield lawyer. By the 1850s the Midwest was honeycombed by railroads and telegraph lines, much more dense than those in the South, and was growing rapidly with surging economic growth and the influx of immigrants, particularly from Germany. It was laced with colleges such as Oberlin,

Hillsdale, and Ohio Central (the alma mater of Warren G. Harding), which admitted women and blacks in antebellum America. It was full of educated people who read the great bestseller of the decade, *Uncle Tom's Cabin* by Harriet Beecher Stowe, who lived in Cincinnati, on one of the Midwest's borders with the slave states.

That leads us to the second crucial date of an extreme event in midwestern history: 1854, the year the Republican Party was established in the Midwest. (Ripon, Wisconsin, and Jackson, Michigan, vie for the honor of being regarded as the place of origin.) In the preceding quarter century, the Midwest had been a political battleground between Andrew Jackson's Democrats and Henry Clay's Whigs, with frontier counties generally voting Democratic while the counties settled by New England Yankee-stock pioneers—northern Ohio, southern Michigan, scattered counties in Indiana, and northern Illinois—generally voted Whig. Yankee-stock midwesterners had a yen for reform, including setting up new churches and even new religions such as Mormonism, fighting for women's rights and temperance, and abolishing slavery and capital punishment. In partisan politics, the rapidly growing Midwest was a political battleground. With Ohio casting two-thirds of its popular votes, it went for Andrew Jackson in 1828 and 1832; as other states gained population, William Henry Harrison, the Indiana Whig, carried the region in 1836 and 1840. Democrats won midwestern pluralities in 1844, 1848, and 1852, but third parties opposing slavery extension or slavery itself won 2 percent, 10 percent, and 7 percent of midwestern votes—numbers close to the Democratic margins of victory.

In the whirling, surging 1850s, information traveled instantly via telegraph, and political actors traveled rapidly by railroad. In January 1854, Senator Stephen Douglas of Illinois, seeking an opening for a transcontinental railroad, introduced the Kansas-Nebraska Act, creating territories west of existing states open to slavery by popular vote—so-called popular sovereignty. The next day, a group of his fellow Democrats signed an appeal opposing the document. In February, a coalition of Whigs, Free Soilers, and antislavery Democrats met in Ripon, Wisconsin, and called for forming a new "anti-Nebraska." In March, Douglas's Kansas-Nebraska bill passed the Senate, and in May it passed the House and was signed by President Franklin Pierce. In July, Kansas-Nebraska opponents in Jackson, Michigan, assumed the label Republican and adopted a platform, and similar meetings were held in Ohio, Wisconsin, Indiana, and Vermont. In October, Abraham Lincoln delivered a speech against the Kansas-Nebraska Act in Peoria. The midterm elections, held in different months from state to state, ended with a House of Representatives where Republicans outnumbered Democrats 108–83, with 43 members representing other parties, and the House elected a nominally Republican Speaker.

The Republicans' raison d'être was to prevent slavery from spreading in the territories. The new party, unlike its opponents the Democrats and its more-or-less predecessor the Whigs, was a northern-only party, distributing ballots and running candidates only in the North, in states where slavery was prohibited. Its policies—including limiting and, within a decade, abolishing slavery; passing a protective tariff to encourage new industry; creating land-grant colleges and the Homestead Act—were inclined to appeal to the highly educated and commercially expanding culture of the Midwest, where the farmer majority made their living exporting crops and livestock over the railroads to the East.

The new Republican Party's nominee, John C. Fremont, failed to carry the Midwest in the party's first presidential election, trailing the Democrat, James Buchanan, by a 46 percent to 43 percent margin. But he carried virtually every county peopled by settlers of New England Yankee stock, and to those the party's 1860 nominee, Abraham Lincoln, added German immigrant counties in Ohio, Indiana, Wisconsin, and Iowa. Lincoln carried the Midwest 49 percent to 43 percent over Stephen Douglas, the Democrat, and by a margin of 66 to 9 electoral votes. For three generations, from 1860 to 1928, Republican presidential nominees carried the midwestern popular vote, with the single exception of 1912, when Theodore Roosevelt, the former president, ran as a Progressive against his Republican successor, William Howard Taft.

The dynamic economy provided Republicans with challenges that they met to the Midwest's satisfaction. The populist movement of the 1890s and the free-silver, inflationary platform of William Jennings Bryan, the Democratic nominee in 1896, yanked the Great Plains states— Kansas, Nebraska, and South Dakota—away from the Republicans. But the adroit response by the Republican nominee, William McKinley[29]— which included the hard-money gold standard, the protective tariff, and openness to labor unions and immigrants—increased Republican support in the fast-growing industrial cities of the Midwest and the Northeast. Republican percentages in the Midwest in the years afterward were higher on average than in the years when memories of the Civil War were fresher (53 percent versus 51 percent).

In the early twentieth century, another component appeared in midwestern political opinion: The region, particularly states such as Wisconsin, Minnesota, Iowa, and the Dakotas with large German and Scandinavian American populations, became the part of the country most skeptical of military action and most inclined toward pacifism, isolationism, and dovishness. In April 1917, 39 of the 56 votes cast against the declaration of war on Germany were cast by senators and representatives from the Midwest, including 10 of the 13 from the most heavily German American state, Wisconsin.

The immediate aftermath of the war was characterized by enormous disorder and disillusion: steep inflation and deep recession, Communist and terrorist attacks such as the bombing of Wall Street, labor union strikes and race riots, and the debate and defeat in the Senate of Woodrow Wilson's Versailles Treaty. This disillusion, as Jon Lauck has written in *From Warm Center to Ragged Edge* and Fred Siegel in *The Revolt Against the Masses*,[30] resulted in a revulsion among intellectuals and writers against middle-class America and against the progressivism they had only recently believed in. This turn was notable especially in the journalism of the antiwar, anti-Prohibition H. L. Mencken and in postwar fiction. Sinclair Lewis made sport of the midwestern small town in *Main Street* and *Babbitt*, while F. Scott Fitzgerald and Ernest Hemingway almost totally ignored the midwestern places where they grew up as rich kids—Fitzgerald on Summit Avenue in St. Paul, Minnesota, and Hemingway in Oak Park, the Chicago suburb where Frank Lloyd Wright was designing dozens of houses that are now tourist attractions.

This revolt showed a contempt for many of the advances of Midwest civilization set in motion by the Northwest Ordinance of 1787 and the Yankee reformist impulse of which the creation of the Republican Party was only one manifestation. It was also hostile to the two most recent products of that impulse, enshrined in the Constitution—the 18th Amendment, prohibiting liquor, and the 19th Amendment, enfranchising women (as South Dakota, Illinois, and Michigan had already done). In effect, the intellectuals were spurning the midwestern culture that promoted education, advanced equal rights for blacks and women, and encouraged family stability, hard work, delayed gratification, and civic involvement. There was also a mostly forgotten encouragement of high culture (Harry Truman took piano lessons from a teacher who had been taught by Ignace Jan Paderewski; the great Civil War historian of one generation, Bruce Catton, grew up in Benzonia, Michigan; and the great Civil War historian of the next, James McPherson, grew up in Valley City, North Dakota). But these achievements were not renounced by the midwestern voters, who in the 1920s rallied to the Republican Party. Its presidential nominees won 64 percent of its votes in 1920, 56 percent in 1924 (when Robert LaFollette, the antiwar senator from Wisconsin, ran as a Progressive and won 20 percent in the region), and 61 percent in 1928. The Midwest remained more Republican than the national average, as it had been since 1856.

Which leads us to the third and final date of an extreme event that I claim was decisive in forming midwestern political attitudes—1937. The Great Depression swung the Midwest away from the Republican Party; the region voted 56 percent to 41 percent for Franklin Roosevelt in 1932, and 58 percent to 38 percent in 1936, giving him all 161 of its electoral votes both times. Just a month after his second victory, in December 1936, workers in General Motors factories in Flint, Michigan, stopped working and occupied the factories. This was the first of multiple sit-down strikes, entirely illegal but tolerated by New Deal Democratic governors in Michigan, Ohio, and Illinois. The industrial union organizers acted rapidly, fearing that the Supreme Court would overturn the Wagner National Labor Relations Act encouraging unionization. But the Court upheld the legislation, and suddenly all the workers in the giant auto, steel, rubber, and agricultural implement factories were represented by the giant United Auto Workers (UAW), United Steelworkers, United Rubber Workers, and Congress of Industrial Organizations unions.

The union victory was not universally popular among midwestern voters. The Democratic governors who declined to stop the sit-down strikers were repudiated in their next elections. Midwest-born Republican candidates ran even in the Midwest against Franklin Roosevelt in the next two presidential elections: The Hoosier-born Wendell Willkie lost the region by just a 49.8 percent to 49.7 percent margin in 1940. Thomas Dewey, a native of Owosso, Michigan, carried the region by 50 percent to 49 percent in 1944, as the isolationist tilt of much of the Midwest worked against the internationalist Democratic president. Harry Truman of Independence, Missouri, carried the Midwest by 50 percent to 48 percent in 1948, as he rallied farm-county voters by arguing that Republicans would cut farm subsidies.

The Midwest continued voting more Republican than the national average, but by decreasing margins, up through and including the 1960 election. But as farm territory lost population and factory cities and towns grew, the region's Republican tilt slackened. Voters in union households, 40 percent of the electorate in Michigan when I was growing up there in the 1950s, tended to align with the union's Democratic politics. Even when union membership started declining in the 1970s, the percentage of voters who grew up in union households, or whose parents did—perhaps 40 percent of today's midwesterners—were inclined in that direction as well. Starting in 1972, the Midwest voted more Democratic or only microscopically more Republican than the national average in every presidential election but one—an exception that proves the rule. In 1976, Republicans nominated Gerald Ford, from Grand Rapids, to run against the Deep South's Jimmy Carter, and the cultural disjunction between the Midwest and the South—apparent since the 1850s—helped Ford carry the region 50 percent to 48 percent and its electoral votes by 87 to 58.

Let me pass over the presidential elections from 1972 to 2004 by simply noting that the Midwest voted much like the nation, usually just a little bit more Democratic, and examine the past three presidential elections, in which the Midwest has once again become more distinctive politically as a region. Below the presidential level, Democrats actually made significant gains in congressional and state legislature elections in the 1970s and 1980s. To the safe Democratic seats in major metropolitan areas, they added significant numbers of seats in what I will call the outstate Midwest (an adjective commonly used in Michigan, although not in other states): the counties outside the major metropolitan areas. Democrats elected a majority of Midwest House members in every election from 1974 to 1992, with the single (and bare) exception of 1980. These victories owe something to the superior political entrepreneurship of Democratic candidates and also something to midwesterners' insistence on honesty, which you can see in the Democratic trend there as the Watergate scandal unfolded. In a 1974 special election, a Democrat even won the Grand Rapids House seat held by Republicans since 1912 and by Gerald Ford for 25 years, which helped lead the way to Richard Nixon's resignation six months later.

These Democratic victories also owe something to a spreading of the ideas of the labor movement: to enlarge the welfare state; to increase public spending, especially on education; and to advance civil rights and equal treatment for blacks. The UAW was a particular leader in this last goal. In the 1950s and early 1960s, when national politicians and many other labor leaders kept arm's length from the civil rights movement, the longtime UAW president Walter Reuther took the lead and participated in Martin Luther King's 1963 March on Washington. There is something in common here between the midwestern roots of the Republican Party and the midwestern roots of the industrial union movement: Both set high priority on advancing equal treatment of black Americans.

Barack Obama could not have been elected president of the United States without unusual, almost unprecedented, support in the Midwest. He carried the region's electoral votes by a margin of 97 to 27 and won 54 percent of the popular vote in the Midwest, more than any other Democrat in history except Lyndon Johnson in 1964 and Franklin Roosevelt in 1936 and 1932. His percentage margin over his Republican opponent was larger than Bill Clinton's in 1992 and the same as Clinton's percentage margin in 1996; his Midwest electoral-vote margin, 70, was almost exactly the same as Bill Clinton's, 71, in both those 1990s elections. This outcome was in part a reaction to the recession that began in 2007 and the financial crash of September and October 2008, which evoked responses that might be expected from an electorate steeped in industrial union politics. It was also a result of disillusion and weariness with the Iraq war in the nation's region most inclined toward pacifism, isolationism, and dovishness.

I think there was another factor, although I know no way of proving it: that the Obama victory owed something to the belief of a majority of Americans that it would be a good thing, as a general proposition, if the country elected a black president—an idea that Obama himself has suggested may have something to it. I believe that impulse was particularly strong in the Midwest, thanks to the heritages that can be traced back to the years 1787, 1854, and 1937. It did not just affect the 10 percent of midwestern voters who are black (a couple of points below the national average) who turned out in record numbers and voted 95 percent for Obama, but also some additional quantum of white voters who might not have turned out to vote for a white Democratic candidate.

So these unusual factors, not duplicated since, helped pump up the Democratic Party's standing in the region well above what it had been since 1994. In that year, midwestern voters overturned the Democrats' 62-43 margin in the region's U.S. House seats to a 59-46 Republican margin, and there were similar reverses in midwestern legislatures as well. Between 1994 and 2004, Republicans won increasing majorities of Midwest House seats. In 2006 and 2008, Democrats had a 55-45 edge in Midwest seats, but then the pattern reverted to the post-1994 norm, with Republicans winning House majorities of 65-35 in 2010, 59-35 in 2012, and 61-33 in 2014 and 2016. So in this decade Republicans have won a higher percentage of midwestern congressional seats than at any time since the Supreme Court's one-man-one-vote decision in 1964.

In 2012, Obama once again carried the midwestern popular vote, but by a narrower margin of 51 percent to 48 percent, and he won the region's electoral votes 80 to 38 only by shrewd organization in the target states. The midwestern union tradition played some role here: Obama ads made sure to remind voters that Romney was the son of an auto company CEO and that, as the Michigan-based auto companies faced financial crises, he wrote an opinion article to which a *New York Times* editor affixed the title "Let Detroit Go Bankrupt" (November 18, 2008). But beneath the top of the ticket, midwestern voters continued to reject the Obama administration's big-government policies as they had rejected the Clinton administration's in the 1990s. And, to the surprise of many, including Hillary Clinton's campaign strategists, they cast a majority of their votes for Donald Trump in 2016. My thesis today is that the same factors—factors that can be traced back to 1787, 1854, and 1937—which helped Obama carry the Midwest in 2008 and 2012 by an average of 6 percent of the popular vote also helped Trump carry the Midwest in 2016 by 5 percent of the popular vote.

It helps my analysis to divide the Midwest into two roughly equal parts. One is the metropolitan Midwest, consisting of all counties in metropolitan areas of one million or more population (plus heavily Democratic Madison, Wisconsin). Together they have cast 46 percent or 47 percent of midwestern votes in the past four presidential elections. The other is the outstate Midwest, the counties outside those million-plus metro areas, which cast 53 percent or 54 percent of the region's votes in the past four elections.

The metropolitan Midwest contains 80 to 90 percent of the Midwest's black and Hispanic citizens and perhaps a slightly smaller percentage of Asians (who are often found in university towns). It is also the more Democratic region and, in this decade, the more consistent. It contains the large majority of the region's college graduates, a demographic group repelled by Donald Trump, whom it gave significantly lower percentages than it did Mitt Romney. The metropolitan Midwest voted 56 percent to 42 percent for Obama in 2012 and 54 percent to 40 percent for Hillary Clinton in 2016. Obama and Clinton thus carried the region by identical margins in popular votes (almost precisely two million) and in percentage terms (13.6 percent). That was a downtick for the Democratic ticket compared with 2008, but a better showing for Clinton than for John Kerry in 2004.

The outstate Midwest was another story. Obama actually carried it by 89,000 votes, 49.5 percent to 49.0 percent, in 2008. In 2012, Romney won the outstate Midwest 52 percent to 46 percent, not enough to prevent Obama from carrying the whole region's electoral votes 80 to 38. It was another story in 2016. Donald Trump carried the outstate Midwest by 57 percent to 37 percent. That is a much better showing even than George W. Bush's 55 percent to 45 percent victory there in 2004. To be sure, Trump's victory margins in Michigan and Wisconsin were exceedingly narrow, as they were in Pennsylvania, and without the electoral votes of those three states he would have been defeated. But he won them and won the Midwest's electoral votes by an 88 to 30 margin, the best Republican showing since the Ronald Reagan landslide of 1984.

Hillary Clinton's percentage in the outstate Midwest, 37 percent, was low for a Democrat—behind Obama's 46 percent in 2012, further behind his 49 percent in 2008, and significantly behind John Kerry's 44 percent in 2004. All of which came as a surprise to many Democratic strategists and journalistic pundits. Many had faith in a theory that Democrats had an increasing advantage because of the rising percentage of nonwhite voters. But those numbers are not rising much in the Midwest. The black population in Michigan, Ohio, Illinois, and Wisconsin may be

declining, as some blacks return to their ancestral South in search of better economic opportunity and more cultural affinity. In any case, no one
expected that black turnout for a post-Obama Democratic presidential
candidate would reach the heights it did for Obama; and indeed black
turnout fell in Cleveland, Detroit, and Milwaukee. As for Hispanics,
many are noncitizens, and the only midwestern states with more than
10 percent Hispanic population, according to 2015 Census estimates, are
safely Democratic Illinois and safely Republican Kansas and Nebraska.
As for Asians, they are no more than 3 percent of the population in any
midwestern state except the region's most Democratic state, Illinois.

Democrats were also enraptured and deceived by another theory,
the so-called blue wall, a term concocted by journalists who noticed
that a group of states plus the District of Columbia with a total of 242
electoral votes had voted Democratic in every election from 1988 to 2012.
They might have added the six electoral votes of Iowa, which in that
period voted Republican only once, by 1 percent, in 2004. But if they
had done so, they might have noticed that other blue-wall states had
voted Democratic only narrowly in multiple elections, including a trio of
states that were crucial in 2016: Wisconsin, Michigan, and Pennsylvania.
The blue wall, in other words, was dangerously low and permeable in
multiple places.

Clinton strategists may not have noticed their candidate's weakness
in states such as Wisconsin, Michigan, Ohio, and Pennsylvania from
statewide polls; regional samples in such polls have a wide margin of
error, so fluctuations can plausibly be dismissed as meaningless noise
rather than meaningful signals. But a louder signal came from Iowa,
which is in the outstate Midwest—it is the nation's largest state with no
counties in a million-plus metro area. The August 2016 polling in Iowa,
showing Trump gaining on Clinton and then taking the lead, had wider
implications for the Midwest, which the Clinton campaign ignored. The
campaign's 34-year-old master strategist also ignored the advice of Bill
Clinton, who said that blue-collar voters needed more attention, and
refused, in a campaign that spent more than $1 billion, to spend money
on late polling in Michigan and Wisconsin. Oops!

In retrospect, the midwestern heritage factors that worked for
Obama in 2008 and 2012 also worked for Trump—or failed to work
for Clinton—in the outstate Midwest in 2016. The first heritage factor

is the historic support for equal rights for blacks. That did not work for Clinton, and the prospect of electing the first female president, a positive motivator for college-educated baby-boom women, did not attract many others. Clinton lost younger women and non-college women to Bernie Sanders in the primaries, and they did not vote for her in high enough numbers to win the general election. Accusing voters who resisted her appeal of being "deplorables"—as Clinton did at a fundraiser in Manhattan—and racists was not a good tactic for winning over those who had voted for the first black president, or who had many friends they saw in Walmart or at church who did.

The second heritage factor is honesty. Clinton's lies and evasions left her with only 32 percent of voters saying she was honest and trustworthy—an extraordinary liability, more significant in the Midwest than in the rest of the country. This is a factor that helped Bernie Sanders in the Democratic primaries and would have helped any Republican opponent in the general election.

Third is the labor-union economic tradition. Trump, like the auto and steel unions for the past forty years and unlike any other Republican nominee in that time, came out against free-trade agreements and lamented the loss of jobs he argued were a result of them. Clinton scrambled to get on the same side of the issue, despite her past stands, but she could not catch up.

The final factor is the Midwest's historical proclivity toward pacifism, isolationism, and dovishness. That helped Obama in 2008, as it had helped Democratic nominees, to varying extents, since the 1980s. But in the 2016 election it was Trump who was decrying the war in Iraq and interventions in the Middle East, and Clinton who was trying to explain why she supported them in the past and was not quite supporting them now.

The result was the first presidential election since 1980 in which the Midwest voted less like the Northeast and the West than like the South. At a time of intense partisan polarization and partisan parity, and in which there has been little change in partisan voting patterns—as little as at any period since the 1880s, arguably—the marked shift in the outstate Midwest, and in the demographically, economically, and culturally similar outstate Pennsylvania and significant parts of Florida, has produced a small but decisive change in popular votes and a major shift of 100 electoral votes, with substantial and as yet not entirely determined changes in public policy. These results raise the question of whether the outstate Midwest is going to make the Midwest as a whole as Republican a region as the South has been in most elections of the past four or five decades.

To that question I have no answer. Donald Trump's presidency could be a great success, a great failure, or something in between. He could become our fourth consecutive president to win a second term—something that has never happened before in American history—or he could be repudiated as one president after another was, in different ways, from 1968 to 1980. It may turn out that he forged a road toward national presidential parties for a Republican Party, whose leaders started off having no use for him. Or it may turn out that his victory was a cul-de-sac, an exception proving the rule, an oddball divergence from the natural order—and that the outstate Midwest could go back to providing crucial votes in electing Democratic presidents, as it did for Barack Obama in 2008 and 2012.

One thing seems clear to me, however, which is that the Midwest, and especially the outstate Midwest, may no longer be ignored by political journalists or taken for granted by Democratic strategists, as it has been after the Iowa caucuses, with the exception of historically marginal Ohio, for lo so many years. For those with a residual affection for the Midwest and a respect for all its admirable historic heritages, that is good news.

ACKNOWLEDGMENTS

I want to thank the Midwestern History Association, Hillsdale College, and The Citadel for invitations to speak on American politics. Thanks also to my colleagues at the American Enterprise Institute and the *Washington Examiner* for stimulating me to think as well as inviting me to write—and for stimulating conversation in the process. And to the many others who over the last half century and more have helped me learn and have on appropriate occasions steered me away from error, many thanks as well.

NOTES

I. The Parties in History

1 Robert Kelley, *The Transatlantic Persuasion: The Liberal-Democratic Mind in the Age of Gladstone* (New Brunswick, N.J.: Transaction, 1969).

2 Karl Rove, *The Triumph of William McKinley: Why the Election of 1896 Still Matters* (New York: Simon & Schuster, 2015).

3 James Grant, *The Forgotten Depression* (New York: Simon & Shuster, 2014), p. 62.

4 Arthur Herman, *1917: Lenin, Wilson, and the Birth of the New World Disorder* (New York: Harper, 2017), p. 419.

5 Conrad Black, *Franklin D. Roosevelt, Champion of Freedom* (New York: PublicAffairs, 2003).

6 Sean Trende, *The Lost Majority: Why the Future of Government Is Up for Grabs—and Who Will Take It* (New York: Palgrave Macmillan, 2012).

II. The Parties in Our Times

7 Sam Rosenfeld, *The Polarizers: Postwar Architects of Our Partisan Era* (Chicago: University of Chicago Press, 2018), pp. 1–10. See also James Bowman, "Parties, Principles, and Polarization," *Weekly Standard*, June 15, 2018.

8 Alan Brinkley, *The End of Reform: New Deal Liberalism in Recession and War* (New York: Knopf, 1995).

9 Sean Trende, "Did JFK Lose the Popular Vote?" Real Clear Politics, October 16, 2012. https://www.realclearpolitics.com/articles/2012/10/19/did_jfk_lose_the_popular_vote_115833-2.html

10   Theodore H. White, *The Making of the President 1960* (New York: Atheneum, 1961).

11   Jay K. Dow, *Electing the House: The Adoption and Performance of the U.S. Single-Member District Electoral System* (Lawrence: University Press of Kansas, 2017), pp. 162–70.

12   Michael Barone, "Ditching Electoral College Would Allow California to Impose Imperial Rule on a Colonial America," *Washington Examiner*, December 6, 2016.

13   Richard B. Cheney and Lynne V. Cheney, *Kings of the Hill: How Nine Powerful Men Changed the Course of American History* (New York: Touchstone, 1996). Also John A. Lawrence, *The Class of '74: Congress after Watergate and the Roots of Partisanship* (Baltimore: Johns Hopkins University Press, 2018).

14   Emphasis on "supposedly." Steven J. Allen debunks this legend in "'We have lost the South for a generation': What Lyndon Johnson said, or would have said if only he had said it," Capital Research Center, October 7, 2014, https://capitalresearch.org/article/we-have-lost-the-south-for-a-generation-what-lyndon-johnson-said-or-would-have-said-if-only-he-had-said-it/

15   See Lawrence, *The Class of '74.*

16   Bill Bishop, with Robert G. Cushing, *The Big Sort: Why the Clustering of Like-Minded Americans Is Tearing Us Apart* (Boston: Houghton Mifflin, 2008).

17   Kiron K. Skinner, Annelise Anderson, and Martin Anderson, eds., *Reagan: In His Own Hand: The Writings of Ronald Reagan That Reveal His Revolutionary Vision for America* (New York: Free Press, 2001).

18   Gene Kopelson, *Reagan's 1968 Dress Rehearsal: Ike, RFK, and Reagan's Emergence as a World Statesman* (Los Angeles: Figueroa Press, 2016).

19   "Adored by so many, he was a man with no real friends." Edmund Morris, "The Unknowable: Ronald Reagan's amazing, mysterious life," *New Yorker*, June 20, 2004. My reading of biographies of Roosevelt and Eisenhower has convinced me that neither of them had any really close friends, anyone he trusted with his innermost thoughts.

20   Charles L. Clapp, *The Congressman: His Work As He Sees It* (Washington, D.C.: Brookings Institution, 1963).

21   John A. Lawrence, "How the 'Watergate Babies' Broke American Politics," *Politico*, May 26, 2018.

22   William Strauss and Neil Howe, *Generations: The History of America's Future, 1584 to 2069* (New York: William Morrow, 1991).

III. The Parties in Regions

23   V. O. Key, Jr., *Southern Politics in State and Nation*, new ed. (1949; Knoxville: University of Tennessee Press, 1984), p. 1.

24   Henry Adams, *History of the United States during the Administration of Thomas Jefferson* (New York: Albert & Charles Boni, 1930), vol. 1, p. 131.

25   David Hackett Fischer, *Albion's Seed* (New York: Oxford University Press, 1989), p. 411.

26   Ibid., p. 777.

27   Sven Beckert, *Empire of Cotton: A Global History* (New York: Knopf, 2014), p. 103.

28   Thomas Bruscino, *A Nation Forged in War: How World War II Taught Americans to Get Along* (Knoxville: University of Tennessee Press, 2010), p. 47.

29   See Karl Rove's excellent book on this underappreciated politician: *The Triumph of William McKinley: Why the Election of 1896 Still Matters* (New York: Simon & Schuster, 2015).

30   Jon K. Lauck, *From Warm Center to Ragged Edge: The Erosion of Midwestern Literary and Historical Regionalism, 1920–1965* (Iowa City: University of Iowa Press, 2017); Fred Siegel, *The Revolt Against the Masses: How Liberalism Has Undermined the Middle Class* (New York: Encounter Books, 2014).

INDEX